D0064673

Fearless Female
SOLDIERS, EXPLORERS, AND AVIATORS

Mae C Jemison

FIRST AFRICAN AMERICAN
WOMAN IN SPACE

KRISTIN THIEL

Cavendish
Square
New York

Published in 2018 by Cavendish Square Publishing, LLC
243 5th Avenue, Suite 136, New York, NY 10016

First Edition

Website: cavendishsq.com

CPSIA Compliance Information: Batch #CS17CSQ

All websites were available and accurate when this book was sent to press.

Library of Congress Cataloging-in-Publication Data

Names: Thiel, Kristin, 1977- author.
Title: Mae C. Jemison : first African American woman in space / Kristin Thiel.
Description: New York : Cavendish Square Publishing, [2018] |
Series: Fearless female soldiers, explorers, and aviators |
Includes bibliographical references and index.
Identifiers: LCCN 2017003657 (print) | LCCN 2017006421 (ebook) |
ISBN 9781502627513 (library bound) | ISBN 9781502627520 (E-book)
Subjects: LCSH: Jemison, Mae, 1956—Juvenile literature. |
African American women astronauts–Biography–Juvenile literature. |
Astronauts–United States–Biography–Juvenile literature.
Classification: LCC TL789.85.J46 T47 2018 (print) | LCC TL789.85.J46 (ebook) |
DDC 629.450092 [B] –dc23
LC record available at https://lccn.loc.gov/2017003657

Editorial Director: David McNamara
Editor: Stacy Orlando
Copy Editor: Nathan Heidelberger
Associate Art Director: Amy Greenan
Designer: Stephanie Flecha
Production Coordinator: Karol Szymczuk
Photo Research: J8 Media

Printed in the United States of America

Contents

one

Jemison's Corner of the Universe

"Don't let anyone rob you of your imagination, your creativity, or your curiosity. It's your place in the world; it's your life." —Mae C. Jemison

In 1992, **astronaut** Mae C. Jemison blasted off into the sky and left this planet. The vessel she rode in shook as though in an earthquake and then ripped through the atmosphere. It only metaphorically tore the air, but that is the most accurate way of describing a vehicle moving under 7 million pounds (3.18 million kilograms) of thrust. Bursting free of Earth's gravitational pull, the *Endeavour* settled, drifting across the

Opposite: A 1992 NASA photo of Jemison, taken before she became the first African American woman in space

starry canvas, and crew member Jemison became the first African American woman in space.

Her ship, the *Endeavour*, was named for an eighteenth-century ship that was one of the first to ride the waves of Earth's Pacific Ocean. When the first *Endeavour* made its monumental, but earthbound, voyage, Africans in the Western world were imprisoned as slaves. Aboard its twentieth-century descendent, Jemison was a highly educated doctor, leader, and regarded astronaut.

Since her childhood, Jemison had the desire to go to space. Perhaps more than any of her defining characteristics—intelligent, determined, strong, kind, generous, and fun-loving—she is intensely curious, wanting to know where we came from, who we are, where we're going—and why. This perspective could be seen in her space career and also in her accomplishments following her journey to space. Her curiosity extended in diverse directions. Jemison holds nine honorary doctorates, and in addition to her role as an astronaut, she has been a physician, scientist, dancer, teacher, activist, entrepreneur, and even an actor on one of the most popular television shows of all time. She left **NASA** six months after her one and only **mission** into space because she felt there was even more for her to do in the world.

The Color of Space Exploration

NASA astronauts were predominately white men in 1992, which is not surprising since white men dominated most of the American military and scientific professions. As a woman and an African American, Jemison's accomplishment is groundbreaking, and what she did undoubtedly led to changed perceptions, expectations, and possibilities. Since the United States has long been a world superpower, including in the **space race**, it does matter when the country makes advancements. It is tempting to assume the first African American woman in space marked the end of discrimination in space exploration around the world, but we shouldn't be lulled into thinking that Jemison's accomplishment illustrates the United States was the principal country to make that leap. There were multiple occasions for minorities to make waves at NASA before they eventually were allowed to do so. The racism and sexism prevalent in the United States prevented the country from leading the world in having a diverse space program.

In fact, the United States was not the first country to send a woman to space—that honor belongs to the former Soviet Union (USSR), which sent Valentina Tereshkova into orbit in 1963. That was a full twenty years before the United States would send its first woman astronaut, Sally Ride, in 1983. Additionally, the United States was not the first country to send a person of African descent into space. The Soviet Union, along with Cuba, again holds that place of distinction. Arnaldo Tamayo Méndez, a Cuban air force pilot of African descent, went to space in 1980 as part of by the Intercosmos **program**, which opened room in Soviet space missions to people of countries politically aligned with the USSR. The first African American into space, Guion Bluford, wouldn't have his chance till 1983.

Interestingly, the United States could have been the first country to step outside the white male box. American women worked in the space industry since its start in the 1940s; even African American women played major roles in NASA from early in the space agency's history. In 1962, President John F. Kennedy selected the first African American to train as an astronaut.

More information about these pioneers is given later in this book, but in short, sexism and racism are powerful obstacles that many individuals had to overcome in the United States.

When she took her first steps toward her goal of visiting space, Jemison realized that she was on the path to becoming not only an astronaut but a role model as well. Jemison hoped that her success as a woman and as a person of color would honor those who lived before her and who, due to discrimination, were not able to follow their dreams. Jemison's success would also be inspirational to others and instill confidence that one could accomplish more than previously imagined. Giving peace to the past and supporting the future, Jemison would help change today's society for the better.

The State of Race on the Eve of Jemison's Birth

Jemison, born in 1956, came of age in the 1960s and 1970s, during great shifts in public policy and public perception on a variety of social issues, including equality for African Americans and women. Of course, change does not happen overnight, so though she grew up in a modernizing era, remnants from years past continued to affect her world. Race relations, for one, were heavily directed by the past, and people were still fighting for future change.

By the mid-1900s, segregation laws and social expectations for racial separation in the United States were under renewed scrutiny and debate. In some cases, legalized racism was overturned, but making integration a reality was messy. Conditions had always been horrific for many people of color, but they seemed to be uniquely challenging during this time.

As minorities finally began to receive opportunities whites had always claimed, they faced new levels of discrimination. For the purposes of this book, about an African American female pioneer, the focus will be on obstacles faced specifically by African Americans and women, but it's crucial to keep in mind that discrimination against many groups in the United States has been pervasive, systemic, legalized, and even enforced.

Some policies had been changed for the better by the time Jemison was born. In 1941, civil rights and labor leaders threatened to stage massive protests against the discriminatory practices of the war-related industries which, although experiencing growth during World War II, were still not training or employing minority groups. In response, President Franklin Roosevelt signed Executive Order 8802, which established the Fair Employment Practices Commission (FEPC). In 1943, because of Executive Order 9346, the commission was twelve regional offices strong, and the staff, working with civil rights leaders, used negotiations and pressure about being patriotic during the war effort to encourage businesses to follow fair employment practices. None of this had legal enforcement; participating in nondiscriminatory hiring practices was still voluntary. But the orders and commission paved the way for African Americans to be hired for more skilled and diverse jobs than they previously could access.

At the same time, Jim Crow laws, named after a song from the 1800s that negatively stereotyped blacks, continued. These acts of government-sanctioned oppression and segregation were devastating not only to African Americans, impacting them physically, emotionally, and financially, but also to the country as a whole, since it can be argued that the laws kept the United States in a backward mindset and prevented full utilization of human potential. Jim Crow laws started around 1865. After the 1896 Supreme Court case *Plessy v. Ferguson* upheld segregation and "separate but equal" facilities, the discriminatory laws and practices lasted legally through a good portion of the next century. Government and police enforced both the laws and social customs of separation.

Civilians also acted on their own to maintain this status quo; participating in violence against African Americans or simply saying nothing in the face of discrimination both allowed Jim Crow to continue. An example of this discrimination was that many blacks who had gotten great jobs thanks to the FEPC were nonetheless stationed in separate offices and forced to use separate cafeterias and bathrooms than whites working the very same jobs. Additionally, African Americans were promoted only so far, or not at all, and were paid less than their white counterparts. Employers used clues on résumés to ascertain a potential employee's race. West Virginia State University, Howard University, and Hampton Institute were all African American schools. Employers could choose not to interview applicants from those schools. African Americans were considered equal to whites only to a degree.

The Age of Change

When Jemison was almost seven years old, laws continued to change, and American society flexed and bowed even more. The Equal Pay Act of 1963 mandated that women and men be paid the same amount for comparable work; President John F. Kennedy signed this act in response to women making, at the time, fifty-nine cents to every dollar men made. The Civil Rights Act of 1964 prohibited discrimination, and it promised equality in the workplace by threatening states with lawsuits by the US Justice Department if discriminatory practices against women and racial minorities continued.

Although everyone theoretically was allowed to vote—black men since the Fifteenth Amendment in 1870, and women since the Nineteenth Amendment in 1920—that wasn't necessarily the case in practice. Poll taxes, which charged people money to vote, as well as literacy tests voters were required to take, disproportionately affected African Americans negatively. That this **disenfranchisement** hit black voters the hardest was not accidental. Once African Americans were legally allowed to vote, many whites tried to do whatever they could to prevent them from doing so. The Voting Rights Act of 1965 put a stop to those practices. Meanwhile, even though previous legal decisions should have made it unnecessary, Title IX of 1972 made illegal discrimination based on sex by any institution or program receiving federal funding. Title IX also played a major role in affecting the landscape of schools.

The modern-day United States still has yet to achieve equality for all. The pay gap is smaller, but wages remain far from equal. In 2015, the Institute for Women's Policy Research reported that women received eighty cents to every dollar a man was paid. Around the presidential elections in 2008, 2012, and 2016, studies found issues of ballot tampering and understaffed polling places, among other concerns, in predominantly African American and Latino neighborhoods. If disparity continued so many years after the passage of the equality acts, it is reasonable to assume that not much had changed during Jemison's adolescence and that she was affected by formalized and casual racism and sexism.

Protests About Race

With new laws and old attitudes trying to exist together, the 1960s were heavy with protests and riots over racial and gender inequality. Martin Luther King Jr. and the Southern Christian Leadership Conference looked to Jemison's childhood home city of Chicago as a northern base from which to expand their civil rights work. The Chicago Freedom Movement began in July 1965, when King arrived by invitation of local civil rights workers to lead a demonstration against unfair education, housing, and employment practices. He saw that while racism could be masked in the North, it was just as prevalent there as it was in the South. He knew it was vital that he demonstrate and that nonviolent methods could work there, too.

Peaceful protests and marches, as well as the formation of projects such as Operation Breadbasket, which worked to end discriminatory hiring practices, continued until violence erupted on August 5, 1966, during a march through an all-white Chicago neighborhood. Residents threw things at the protestors, and King himself was hit by a rock.

Protests for Women's Rights

People were also fighting for women's rights. In 1967, the National Organization for Women (NOW) picketed the *New York Times* to protest the newspaper's gender-segregated help-wanted ads. Take Back the Night events, which are held worldwide and shed light on sexual assault and other violence against women, began in 1973 under NOW's leadership. Starting with a march in Illinois's state capital of Springfield in May 1976, people fought across the nation with renewed vigor for the passage of the Equal Rights Amendment (ERA), which was originally drafted in 1923 to nationally guarantee rights for women. Some of the biggest marches drew one hundred thousand people (Washington, DC, 1978) and ninety thousand people (Chicago, 1980). People are still lobbying for passage of the ERA.

NASA Desegregation

Around this time, Jemison's future field of **aerospace** was also rumbling with the pull of old ways and the push of progress. In March 1961, not even two months into his presidency, John F. Kennedy signed Executive Order 10925, requiring government agencies not to discriminate in their hiring. This should have had an exciting effect on the space industry, which was one of the government's fastest growing departments and was located in the region of the country most hostile toward African Americans, the South. Though federal law had changed, individual attitudes, including how local law officials behaved, didn't necessarily change. Still, several black men applied for and received jobs soon after the passage of this new order.

As a black man living in a legally discriminatory society, Julius Montgomery knew that taking a job at Cape Canaveral in Orange County, Florida, wouldn't be easy. For one, the local sheriff and several councilmen were known members of the Ku Klux Klan. Yet Montgomery became one of the first black professionals working in the US space program. Montgomery's coworkers wouldn't even speak to him. Prior to Montgomery, it was reported that the only African Americans employed at Cape Canaveral were janitors.

Morgan Watson also knew there would be challenges when he took a space industry job in Huntsville, Alabama, very near Decatur, where Jemison was born. At a Ray Charles

In 1961, the year this photo was taken, John F. Kennedy signed an executive order promoting equal employment.

concert in town, he found an actual rope dividing the arena, whites on one side and blacks on the other. Both Montgomery and Watson displayed a lot of strength in the face of this strange mix of acceptance and rejection. Jemison would reference Watson's as one of the many stories that are, "like so much of the African-American history, often marginalized and then forgotten."

In the Footsteps of Those Who Came Before

Space exploration is a relatively recent adventure in human history, so not all of Jemison's predecessors are astronauts. Some were **aviators**; others were not aerospace engineers but rather experts in other fields, like math or botany. Each of these professions ultimately supports the advancement of space travel and study.

Even if young Jemison had more role models who were astronauts, she probably still would have taken her inspiration from multiple professions. Jemison views all jobs as components of the same system. "It's important to realize that space exploration is not just astronauts going up on the space **shuttle**," she said in a 2001 online interview, facilitated by Scholastic, with classrooms and students across the country. People who get the shuttle ready, rocket designers, physicians, secretaries, and data analyzers are all crucial to the space program. Astronauts "wouldn't have gotten anywhere, as cool as we think we are, if it wasn't for the technicians and maintenance workers and others who facilitated things," Jemison said to University of Virginia students in 2016 as part of the school's Excellence Through Diversity Distinguished Learning Series. At her Women of Color in Flight gala in 2006, Jemison included many people in the celebration, including her suit tech from her 1992 mission, Sharon McDougle. "She placed me in the same category as the women astronauts," McDougle said in an interview with the NASA Johnson Space Center Oral History Project.

Bessie Coleman: First African American Woman in the Skies

One likely role model for Jemison is Bessie Coleman, known for becoming the first African American and Native American woman to earn an **aviation** pilot's license. She was only thirty-four when she died, thirty years before Jemison's birth. Coleman developed a passion for flight in her early twenties, but every flying school she applied to rejected her on the basis of both race and gender. Robert Abbott, the founder and owner of the newspaper the *Chicago Defender*, and one of the first African American millionaires, encouraged her to keep trying in France, where women could fly professionally. It was there Coleman was finally able to earn her license.

Though she'd been snubbed by pilots and aviation schools before, Coleman returned to the United States in

Bessie Coleman posing with a plane, circa 1922

1921 a celebrity. Reporters met her at the airport. She was a Chicagoan at the time, just like Jemison would be, and her accomplishment was publicized in the *Defender*. She was invited to be the guest of honor at events; at a performance of the musical *Shuffle Along*, the entire audience, including those who were white, gave her a standing ovation.

Coleman earned her living **barnstorming** and performing feats of **aerobatics**. Her long-term plan was to open a flight school that would accept women and people of color. She spoke passionately on rights for African Americans and did what she could to condemn discriminatory practices, including refusing to perform at events that did not allow African American participants, patrons, or attendees. In April 1926, Coleman died tragically in a plane crash. Ten thousand people paid their respects at her funeral, which was led by Ida B. Wells, a prominent civil rights journalist and activist.

The Human Computers

During Jemison's astronaut days, computers were common, but had she flown a few decades earlier, a special group of individuals with amazing computation abilities would have been part of the team with which she shared a spotlight. Some of these "human computers" were African American women.

There are so many variables to launching a shuttle into space and landing it safely back on Earth. Brilliant mathematical minds were needed to make all sorts of calculations for NASA missions, including what day and time a shuttle should blast off in order to fly the most accurate **trajectory** for getting where it's scheduled to go.

Sweet Home Chicago

Though Jemison was born in Decatur, Alabama, she considers Chicago, Illinois, her home, since her family moved there when she was three years old. According to population statistics gathered by the 1960 US census, Chicago was the second-largest city in the nation when the family arrived there, with more than 3.5 million residents. Located along major water transit corridors, it's long been a hub of industry, drawing people in for work.

A quarter of the population was African American; Chicago was one of the cities to which Southern African Americans moved in search of better lives, though they didn't necessarily find improvement. In response to the migration, whites clustered in certain neighborhoods and the suburbs, leaving African American residents to the poor neighborhoods of the "Black Belt" of the South Side, where Jemison's family lived. Eventually, neighborhoods were destroyed and massive public housing units were built, furthering problems of violence and crime. In her "Daring Makes a Difference" lecture, part of the 2016 Extraordinary Women lecture series at Auburn University, Jemison said she was regularly reminded of her "place" as an African American female, and that place was well below the station of her white counterparts. Chicago remains one of the most segregated cities in the United States.

Though racism has long been an ugly, destructive force in the city, Chicago has also been home to impressive firsts by African Americans. Jean Baptiste Point du Sable, a black man

Downtown Chicago in the 1960s looked like this view when Mae Jemison moved there as a preschooler.

from what is now Haiti, is considered the city's first permanent resident, aside from the Miami, Sauk, Fox, and Potawatomi tribes who had lived in the area at various times over the centuries. Poet Gwendolyn Brooks, who, like Jemison, moved to Chicago when she was young (Brooks was originally from Topeka, Kansas), won a Pulitzer Prize in 1950, becoming the first African American to receive this top literary honor; she was also the state's poet laureate and the first African American woman to be appointed as the country's consultant in poetry to the Library of Congress. In the 1980s, Harold Washington was elected twice as the city's mayor (he died in office during his second term), being the first African American to hold that position. He was instrumental earlier in his political career in establishing Martin Luther King Jr.'s birthday as a holiday. His home state of Illinois was, in fact, the first in the nation to declare it an official holiday.

Three of NASA's human computers in 1950 (*from left to right*): Dorothy Vaughan, Leslie Hunter, and Vivian Adair

NASA likes to work with Earth's natural speed and direction in order to give the shuttle an extra boost and save fuel in the process. Earth travels around the sun at about 67,000 miles per hour (107,800 kilometers per hour) and spins eastward on its axis at about 1,000 miles per hour (1,600 kmh). That's power worth using, but the calculations don't stop there. A shuttle doesn't just leave a spinning object; it also tries to land on or meet up with another moving object, which is moving at a different speed than Earth. NASA suggests a neat at-home experiment to explain how difficult it is to understand how all these moving pieces can work together effectively.

In order to gain an understanding of all the moving variables, you could try the following experiment. Bring a container of tennis balls, golf balls, or wadded-up pieces of paper and an empty bucket to a park where there's a playground merry-go-round (the kind you manually push). Set the empty bucket about 9 feet (2.7 meters) from the merry-go-round. Leave the carousel motionless and step on it. Throw a few balls into the empty bucket, then push, or have someone else push, the merry-go-round. Now that you're spinning, try hitting the bucket target. You may miss more often than you did when you were standing still; you at least have to think more and time your throw. Now imagine if your bucket target was also on a spinning platform.

Human computers like Katherine Johnson figured out how to get the shuttle (the ball) to the right place in space (the bucket), calculating backward from the desired end result. Without Johnson and her colleagues, American astronauts wouldn't have gotten into space or walked on the moon.

Katherine Johnson

Katherine Johnson was born on August 26, 1918, two years before the August 26, 1920, ratification of the Nineteenth Amendment, which granted women voting rights. She was born more than fifty years before the 1971 creation of Women's Equality Day, also August 26, celebrating the ratification. Her parents raised her and her siblings with an emphasis on education and encouraged her to embrace her abilities. It was as though her parents knew Johnson had been born on a date that would signify equality across genders. In fact, to help his daughter continue her education past grade school, Johnson's father moved the family 120 miles (193 km) across West Virginia, to a high school that would accept her. The fact that he didn't want her to call a grade school education

Carol Moseley Braun: First African American Female Senator

The year Jemison became the first African American woman in space, Carol Moseley Braun became the first African American woman to be elected to the US Senate. Moseley Braun and Jemison were contemporaries, the former born almost exactly nine years before the latter, and were both raised in Chicago.

Moseley Braun's history-making political race was a tough one. In the Democratic primaries, she beat Alan Dixon, the incumbent in the Senate office, who was expected to continue to win. She went on to make history in the 1992 election, triumphing over Richard S. Williamson, her Republican opponent, even though he raised concerns about the way she handled a tax situation. Allegations were made, and though no charges were ever filed, scandal continued to affect her. Claims that she misused campaign funds during that 1992 election played at least some role in her not being reelected in 1998.

Though Moseley Braun tried to better the world through political channels, being a politician was never her end goal. Improving society was. As a child, she staged a one-person sit-in at a restaurant that would not serve her; later, she marched with Martin Luther King Jr. When Moseley Braun left the Illinois House of Representatives, before her national Senate run, her fellow state representatives named her Conscience of the House. Her legislative initiatives while a US senator included

Carol Moseley Braun in 2004, twelve years after she became a US senator from Illinois

an Education Infrastructure Act, the Women's Pension Equity Act, and historic preservation for important Underground Railroad sites.

Sitting on a panel in 2014 to recognize African American senators, Moseley Braun summarized the challenge of being an African American woman pioneer in any field. "Somebody once asked me which is worse," she said, referring to discrimination based on race or based on gender. She continued, as reported by the *Washington Post*, "My response to that is, if someone has their foot on your neck, it doesn't really matter why it's there."

good enough was something special in that era. Schools suffered during the Great Depression, which lasted a decade, beginning in 1929, when Johnson was eleven. By 1933, when Johnson was high-school aged, 2.2 million children were out of school because of funding cuts. Two thousand schools in rural areas, such as West Virginia, closed. Legal racial segregation added to Johnson's obstacles. In 1930, 15 percent of adult African Americans living in rural parts of the country had no formal schooling, and 48 percent hadn't gone to junior high, let alone high school, as Johnson did. In 1932, 230 counties in the South did not offer high schools for black students but did for whites.

Good in all subjects, but especially buoyed by her innate ability with math, Johnson graduated from high school at age fourteen, and college at eighteen. This was only 1936, so despite her brilliance, she was still unjustly hindered by society's perception of her race and gender. Her career options were limited until 1953, when the most surprising of opportunities came along for Johnson: she became a computer for the space industry.

The National Advisory Committee for Aeronautics (**NACA**), what would become NASA in 1958, started hiring women for technical jobs in 1935. This was during the height of World War II, when men were fighting overseas, and employers at home needed workers. The agency even hired African American women, and NACA was happy with their work. Even after the men returned from the war, NACA kept the women around for a practical reason: demand for qualified people was growing.

Space exploration was kicking into high gear, and there was a lot of new work to be done. In four years, Langley Research Center's Guidance and Navigation Department grew from

500 employees to 1,500, and there was need for more. "Closets and hallways, stockrooms and model shop floors stood in as makeshift offices," Margot Lee Shetterly writes in her book *Hidden Figures: The American Dream and the Untold Story of the Black Women Mathematicians Who Helped Win the Space Race.* "Someone came up with the bright idea of putting two desks head to head and jury-rigged the new piece of furniture with a jumpseat, in order to squeeze three workers into space designed for two."

Johnson was soon promoted to a previously all-male flight research team, where she calculated the trajectory for the flight of the first American in space, Alan Shepard, in 1961. Not quite a year later, NASA would be relying on electronic computers to calculate trajectories, but John Glenn asked Johnson to double-check those numbers by hand for his historic flight that year. With her help, he successfully became the first American to orbit Earth. In a stunning feat, especially for an African American woman at that time, she worked on the *Apollo 11* mission, which in 1969 put humans on the moon for the first time.

President Barack Obama, the first African American president of the United States, presented Johnson with the Presidential Medal of Freedom, the highest award the president can give a civilian, in 2015. In 2016, Johnson was recognized by Hollywood: she was featured in an episode of the NBC television series *Timeless* that year. Then, in early 2017, a movie adaptation of Shetterly's *Hidden Figures* was released, starring Taraji P. Henson as Johnson, and Octavia Spencer and Janelle Monáe as Dorothy Vaughan and Mary Jackson, the other two women highlighted in Shetterly's book.

two

Early Life on Earth

> "Growing up [on the] South Side of Chicago I was just like every other kid; I loved space, stars, and dinosaurs." —Mae C. Jemison

Jemison was born on October 17, 1956, to Charlie, a roofer, maintenance worker, and cab driver, and Dorothy, an elementary school teacher. She was her parents' third and final child; sister Ada and brother Charles, nicknamed Ricky, were born first. Her first name is her mother's middle name. The maternity ward nurses called newborn Jemison by the name Rosebud, for her natural pucker, and her father nicknamed her Fattening Bug because she grew quickly.

Opposite: Even from a young age, Mae Jemison looked like she was destined for greatness.

Decatur, Alabama, where Jemison was born, is also her mother's hometown. Her father was from Talladega, Alabama, about 140 miles (225 km) southwest of Decatur. His ancestors were slaves in Talladega County and stayed on in the area as freed laborers and servants after emancipation. Life there was difficult for many reasons. People who had once been slaves could not find other work, even though the law said they were free. Discrimination remained, and former slaves had no money, education, or work experience outside of the tasks they'd been forced to perform. Also, they had established communities in the same areas where they had been enslaved. Seven years after the signing of the Emancipation Proclamation by President Abraham Lincoln and five years after what would come to be known as Juneteenth, the date when all slaves had finally been told they were free, the US census records of 1870 showed forty-seven black or mixed-race people living near where the Jemison family had been enslaved. By participating in the 2006 PBS television program *African American Lives*, Jemison learned she was 13 percent East Asian.

When Jemison was a toddler, her family moved to Chicago, and from there, she explored the world—and eventually the universe.

Curiosity

Jemison has called herself a scaredy-cat, citing her childhood fear of the dark when her older siblings locked her in the basement, and her fear of heights when she had to ride the El, Chicago's elevated train that at some stations runs high above the ground. Yet those are standard fears that could be considered minor. Where it counts, Jemison has always had guts. She was born with a strong curiosity and sense of self. She may have feared the dark and heights, but she wasn't scared to express herself, even when individuals and society told her she couldn't be all that she wanted to be.

An early example of this was when she was two years old—and drove her father's car. Many people have stories of climbing into the driver's seat when their parents leave the car unattended for just a moment. That was what happened with Jemison when her dad stepped away to help her mom load groceries into the car, but there was a twist. Charlie's Buick was a manual, not an automatic. Jemison didn't just put the car in gear; she somehow managed to pop the clutch, put the car into gear, and hit the gas. Perhaps not only her curiosity but her mechanical aptitude was showing.

The Importance of Education

As a railway midpoint of Nashville, Tennessee, and Mobile, Alabama, as well as Chattanooga, Tennessee, and New Orleans, Louisiana, and situated along both Wheeler Lake and the Tennessee River, Jemison's birthplace of Decatur was a hub for transportation. With the space race increasing in pace and intensity, nearby Huntsville, Alabama, home of the Marshall Space Flight Center, was pushing Decatur out of its place of importance. (Huntsville was even called Rocket City.) Yet more opportunities for the family lay to the north. For one thing, Jemison's mother wanted to finish her college education; she would do so, as well as eventually earn her master's degree. Consequently, when Jemison was three years old, the family moved more than 700 miles (1,126 km) from Decatur, Alabama, to Chicago, Illinois, in search of better prospects and better education.

In 1964, five full years after the Jemisons left the South for the Midwest, the Coleman Report, made possible by the Civil Rights Act of 1964, found that 87 percent of white high school seniors scored higher in math and reading than the average black senior. The biggest gap between races was in the South. It was a terrifying realization. Interestingly, by 2013, that large gap in the South had narrowed, with black and white students performing in math and reading nearly equally, while in the Midwest, to which the Jemisons had moved fifty years before, the gap between blacks and whites in reading ability had widened.

A Young Scientist

At Woodlawn Elementary School, Jemison's kindergarten teacher asked her students what they each wanted to be when they grew up. The teacher was shocked when Jemison said she wanted to be a scientist. In 1961, women and African Americans were not usually scientists. Even when her teacher suggested that she meant she wanted to be a nurse, a profession "acceptable" for females, Jemison persisted, saying again that she would be a scientist. Fortunately, a few years later, one of her teachers would encourage her in science; sixth-grade teacher Mrs. Miller even got a shout-out by Jemison in 2015. Jemison shared in her "Daring Makes a Difference" lecture that she didn't reject things that were traditionally for girls—she played with Barbies just like most little girls did then, but she also played with chemistry sets. That optimism that she could be whatever she wanted made her unique.

Jemison certainly seemed to have the patience of a scientist. Her first research project lasted three years, from grade three to grade six. She conceived of it and designed it for herself. Reading after school and on breaks at the library, she studied the different eras of time, such as the Mesozoic, when dinosaurs lived, and the Cenozoic, when humans live.

Jemison knew she wanted to be a scientist even when she was in kindergarten!

She then constructed a diorama for each, representing what the world was like during each era. Another time, she turned an infection from a splinter in her thumb into a detailed study of pus. She was always creating independent projects for herself, some of which were reused ideas from her siblings or finessed with her parents' help.

Jemison didn't only read science texts; she appreciated fiction when a story involved science. Two of her favorite books in sixth grade were Madeline L'Engle's *A Wrinkle in Time* and *The Arm of the Starfish* "because they had women scientists and girl heroines."

When Jemison was ten, her family moved from the Woodlawn neighborhood of Chicago to the Morgan Park neighborhood and became the first African American family on her street. With the move of homes and schools, Jemison also changed what grade she was supposed to be in. Her academic scores were strong enough that she skipped seventh grade and started her new school as an eighth grader.

Hailing Frequencies Open

Role models can be found in many places. They don't even have to be real people in order to be effective in helping someone do something great. Many of our pioneers and leaders have taken inspiration from fictional characters. Sometimes, these imaginary people have done things that society doesn't support real people doing, which encourages change in real life. When Jemison was around ten years old, she found very real inspiration in a fictional character—and that support lasts even through this day!

The television show *Star Trek*, which premiered in 1966, portrays a space ship with a very diverse crew. The show "was one of our most hopeful fantasies," Jemison said in a Makers video interview. "It helped me to say that, yes, [being an astronaut] is something that was reasonable to think about."

Nichelle Nichols played Lieutenant Uhura on *Star Trek*, a groundbreaking television role for African Americans.

(Launched in 2012, Makers is a women's media and leadership platform documenting the stories of women leaders.)

Jemison looked up to Lieutenant Uhura, one of the first African American characters on American television who was not a slave or servant. Uhura was the communications officer and later a lieutenant commander aboard the *Enterprise* on *Star Trek*. She was in a technical role and was fourth in command of a spaceship. Her name means "freedom" in Swahili. When Jemison was working on her spaceship during her 1992 NASA mission, she began each shift with the phrase "hailing frequencies open," Uhura's most famous line.

Chicagoan Nichelle Nichols, who played Uhura through the sixth Star Trek film, hadn't planned to stay with the show past its first television season. Trained in musical theater, she dreamed of a career on Broadway. The weekend she told the show's creator that she was leaving, she attended an NAACP fund-raising event where she met Martin Luther King Jr. He told her that he was her biggest fan and that hers was the only television show that he and his wife would allow their children to stay up late to watch—and they did so because of her. They believed her character could teach their children something positive about being an African American. Nichols told National Public Radio in 2011 that King said to her, "You are marching. You are reflecting what we are fighting for." Nichols knew then that she couldn't quit *Star Trek*, and she changed her mind.

In 1993, Jemison appeared on *Star Trek: The Next Generation* as Lieutenant Palmer. Cast member LeVar Burton (who played the character Geordi La Forge) invited her to be on the show after he learned about her love of the show and appreciation for Nichols's character. With this opportunity, Jemison said to NOVA, she continued the circle: first, Nichols's imagining of an African American woman in space long before that was a reality inspired Jemison and countless others, and then Jemison "got to come back around and verify that, yes, this happens."

High School

At Morgan Park High School, Jemison met more teachers who were disbelieving of her goals. She was the first girl ever to sign up for drafting class. Drafters produce drawings of residential and commercial buildings, bridges, flood-control projects, or circuitry for construction, architecture, **aeronautics**, and electronics. Jemison's brother had taken the course and enjoyed it, and it seemed perfect for her interests. When the teacher saw her name on the registration list, he contacted her homeroom teacher to ask if the entry was a joke. Jemison was used to this dismissive attitude, and she kept doing as she'd always done: moving onward and upward. In addition to her class load, she was involved with the pom-pom squad and the modern dance troupe. And she continued her at-home experiments. One required her to set bowls of goldfish around the house. The family's cats loved that. Jemison graduated at the young age of sixteen and, with a National Achievement Scholarship to help, started at Stanford University in California that same year.

Stargazing

Jemison "loved to stare up at the stars," she said in an interview with PBS television. "I imagined myself going there." She kept a close eye on news about Project Apollo, learning when all

Ptolemy (*left*), a Greek astronomer and geographer who lived and worked in Egypt, being guided by Urania

the missions were set to happen and what each one's goals were. The manned Apollo missions occurred between 1967 and 1972, when Jemison was ten to sixteen years old.

To have the idea that she could fly to the stars at that time might have felt to some people like an impossibility, and a cruel impossibility for an American woman at that. In 1963, the first woman in space, Soviet **cosmonaut** Valentina Tereshkova, orbited Earth forty-three times. In the United States however, only military jet pilots were considered strong enough to survive traveling through Earth's atmosphere, and only men could be military jet pilots.

Nonetheless, Jemison remained confident in what she could become, and that hopeful optimism alone may have kept her moving toward her goal. To this day, she hates the word "dream." According to Jemison, "It implies something you can't do." In her interview with Scholastic readers, she said that she wished people, especially girls and women, would stop using the word. Instead, she offered, "I like to say, 'What do you intend to do?' So, the question becomes, 'How will you do what you intend to do?'"

She may also have taken some solace in what she'd learned over her years reading books on everything from archaeology to astronomy. From ancient times, there were scientists and astronomers in Mali and the Songhai Empire, both of West Africa, as well as in Egypt. People who looked like Jemison—at least generally, in terms of being from Africa and having brown or black skin—were studying the stars. Even though in college Jemison would find that she'd be the only African American in many of her classes, and despite the perception in America that space was the property of whites alone, Jemison would continue working toward her goal.

College

While still in high school, Jemison attended a two-week Junior Engineering Technical Society program at the University of

Almost the First

Wanting to change the all-white look of NASA in 1962, President John F. Kennedy selected the first African American to train to become an astronaut. US Air Force Captain Ed Dwight came with a stellar background and a recommendation from the National Urban League. In 1933, Dwight was born into prestige in Kansas City. His father played second base with the Negro League, a league for African American professional baseball players until Jackie Robinson disrupted the sport's racial segregation in 1945 and Major League Baseball opened to all races.

After flying for the Air Force as a test pilot, Dwight earned a degree in aeronautical engineering. When Kennedy selected him for the space program, Dwight became the cover story for *Ebony*, *Jet*, and other major publications around the world.

Tragically, Kennedy was assassinated, and the racially charged atmosphere drove Dwight from the program before he had the chance to go into space. According to Dwight, he was reassigned to be a liaison officer in Germany, and he resigned from the Air Force. He worked for a while as an engineer and then earned a master of fine arts degree in 1977. Now he's a well-regarded sculptor, focusing on people and events from American history. His range is wide, looking at both stories of celebration and those of tragedy. For example, as of 2015, he'd crafted seven statues of Martin Luther King Jr. He also created the African American History Monument, a tormented scene from a slave auction. That monument resides at South Carolina's state capitol.

Illinois. This started her thinking about pursuing that scientific path, though she didn't want to give up any of her creative pursuits either. So, at Stanford, she earned a double major.

One degree was in chemical engineering. She said in her 2012 testimony before the Senate Committee on Health, Education, Labor and Pensions that though she is a proud alumna of Stanford's excellent engineering and science programs, she may have earned her engineering degree "in spite of, rather than because of" some of her professors. Many of her math and science instructors gave her a "poor reception," seeming to not want her in their classes. She remembered, during an interview with *Fortune* magazine, that one professor reacted to each question she asked as if it were a dumb point. "And then maybe a white male down the way would ask the same question and he'd tell him, 'That's an astute observation.'"

The other half of her double major took her completely out of the lab: Jemison earned a degree in African and Afro-American studies. As a little bonus, Jemison felt the variety in her classes helped her to recuperate and reenergize. She found her professors outside of math and science welcoming of her (probably because arts, languages, and "soft" sciences have traditionally been seen as subjects for females). So, in those classes, she could "emotionally re-charge and surmount the challenges" of the chilly attitude she faced in the male-dominated departments.

She also continued dancing, and she acted in plays. In 1976, a year before graduation, she represented Stanford at the Caribbean Festival of the Arts in Jamaica. Meanwhile, she was elected head of the Black Student Union. She had served in student government before college, too.

Jemison participated in a lot of things because her interests are diverse. She sees that as a hallmark of true scientists. Scientists are interested in the world, in asking questions about it and understanding how all its components work together. That means, in Jemison's view, wanting to make time to participate in a variety of activities. Jemison is serious about that. When Scholastic readers asked her what classes high school students should take to prepare to become astronauts, she said, "The most important thing is to be well-rounded—you need to know what's going on in the world around you."

She sees artists the same way, curious about everything, and she likes how these two components can work together both in herself and the world. "I think of the physical sciences as our ability to try to understand the world around us, the universe as it's experienced by everyone—and then trying to influence that universe," she said in NOVA's video series *The Secret Life of Scientists and Engineers*. "And I think of the arts as our attempt to have other people understand our personal perspective of the universe. The arts and the sciences … provide a fuller communication together of what and who we are as people."

Dancing

Jemison had the love of dance in common with her role model Nichols. *In Star Trek V*, Nichols had the opportunity to dance for movie audiences when Uhura lured the bad guys away with a performance. Nichols was in her fifties then and was portrayed as gorgeous and powerful. From a young age, Jemison also recognized dance as a way to cultivate her confidence. Jemison has said she "pitched a fit" to get her mother to let her take dance when she was a child. Her

The First African American Astronaut

Jemison was the first African American woman to go into space but not the first African American. Nine years before Jemison went to space, Guion S. "Guy" Bluford Jr. earned that distinction. Bluford became a NASA astronaut in 1979. On August 30, 1983, he went into space aboard the *Challenger*. He went on to fly on three other NASA missions, his last launching December 2, 1992, nearly three months after Jemison became the first African American woman in space. In all, Bluford spent more than 688 hours in space.

He was born November 22, 1942, and raised in Philadelphia, Pennsylvania. His education was extensive, most of it focusing on aerospace engineering, which served him well, first as a US Air Force pilot (he flew 144 combat missions in the Vietnam War) and then as a staff development engineer for the Air Force Flight Dynamics Laboratory.

Bluford acknowledges his role as a model for people such as Jemison, knowing that his success would inspire others and open doors previously closed to African Americans. "But the important thing," he said, as quoted on the New Mexico Museum of Space History website, "is not that I am black, but that I did a good job as a scientist and an astronaut." That perspective is like Jemison's. It is true these astronauts are important African Americans, but they are also extraordinary individuals and scientists, regardless of ethnicity.

Jemison took a poster of Judith Jamison's inspirational performance in Alvin Ailey's *Cry* with her into space.

protest was effective, and she was soon studying African and Japanese styles of dance, ballet, jazz, and modern. She found it exhilarating and fun.

Jemison had been a bit hesitant and shy around people, and anxious in certain situations, but dance helped her confidence grow. It showed her she had power. Other skills she learned through dance translated to her work as an astronaut: She learned to practice constantly, staying diligent and determined. She learned to be precise with her movements and work through physical and mental discomfort and pain. Her memory for sequences improved, since there's a need for retention in everything from learning the various steps and poses to following a routine for a performance. Similarly, there is a lot of memory needed to follow the steps of a procedure exactly to make a space shuttle run correctly.

For her mission into space, Jemison packed a poster of Judith Jamison performing the solo dance *Cry. Cry* details and celebrates the complexity of the experience of the African American woman. Jamison was a star in and eventual artistic director of the Alvin Ailey American Dance Theater in New York City, a premier American dance company since 1958. Jemison herself took modern dance classes there during her years at Cornell Medical School.

Jemison has even danced in space! "It felt very free," she said in a Scholastic interview. She spun an incredible ten times in a row, and she could lift her legs to an extent that she couldn't in full gravity. "I could do wonderful leaps," she said, "*but I didn't come down.*"

Medical School, Peace Corps, and Further Adventures

After graduating from Stanford in 1977, Jemison entered Cornell University Medical School in New York City. Now her extracurricular activities played out on a world stage. Jemison put her skills, abilities, talents, and compassion to work in a variety of settings around the world before she left her twenties. She traveled to Cuba with fellow students to learn about that country's medical system, practices, and techniques. On a grant from the International Travelers Association, she went to Kenya, where she worked with the Flying Doctors, a group that flew to remote areas to provide people with medical care. Between her third and fourth years at Cornell, she worked at a Cambodian refugee camp in Thailand. In her then home of New York City, she organized a citywide health fair as a representative of the National Student Medical Association.

In the early 1980s, Mae Jemison supported Peace Corps volunteers as a medical officer in Sierra Leone and Liberia.

Through her university work and studies, Jemison became fluent in Swahili, Russian, and Japanese. These would serve her well in her work as an astronaut. All astronauts must take Russian language classes, and Jemison's mission to space would be a joint US-Japan venture.

Jemison graduated from Cornell in 1981 and started the next stage of medical training, her internship, at the Los Angeles County/University of Southern California Medical Center. After completing that in July 1982 and finishing out the year as a general practitioner in Los Angeles, she left for Africa again, this time as a part of the Peace Corps.

For two and a half years, from January 1983 through June 1985, Jemison served as a medical officer for Sierra Leone and Liberia in West Africa. She wasn't a Peace Corps volunteer but a staff person. She coordinated the health care, including pharmacy and lab services, for US Peace Corps and US Embassy personnel. She supervised medical staff, wrote heath education curriculum, provided health-related training, and developed and implemented public health and safety guidelines. She said she was on call around the clock to help personnel with physical or mental health concerns. She worked with the National Institutes of Health (NIH) and the Centers for Disease Control and Prevention (CDC) on research projects studying the hepatitis B vaccine, rabies, and schistosomiasis (snail fever, a parasitic disease carried by freshwater snails).

Back in the United States after her Peace Corps service, Jemison worked as a general practitioner and took graduate-level engineering courses. She did this with her eye on a longer-range prize. Even after all the adventures she'd loved having, Jemison later told NOVA, "I still wanted to go into space!"

three

Jemison's Adulthood

"If you have a goal that is very, very far out, and you approach it in little steps, you start to get there faster. Your mind opens up to the possibilities." —Mae C. Jemison

I t could be said that Jemison had been preparing up to this point to make just one call. One day, she picked up the phone ... and called NASA.

"They didn't laugh," she told NOVA of her call to the Johnson Space Center.

Born with a love of science and a lifelong curiosity about everything, she had achieved an impressive résumé that spanned from top-level university degrees through top-level work experience. She applied to be an astronaut.

Opposite: In 1991, Jemison was working for NASA, but she hadn't yet been sent into space.

An Application of a Lifetime

The year 1983, two years before Jemison made that phone call, was a big one for the American space program. As the first American woman in space, Sally Ride dismantled NASA's antiquated rule about females not being suited for space, and Guy Bluford Jr. turned some of society's racial prejudices when he piloted his first mission past Earth's atmosphere. Those two events buoyed Jemison's confidence that the time was right for her involvement.

Jemison submitted her application to NASA in October 1985, but it was not reviewed right away. Astronaut recruitment and selection was put on hold when the space shuttle *Challenger* broke apart just over a minute after launching on January 28, 1986. That mission claimed the lives of several pioneers: Christa McAuliffe, the first civilian selected to go into space; Judith Resnik, who had been the first Jewish American in space two years prior; Ellison Onizuka, the first Asian American astronaut; and Ronald McNair, one of the first African American astronauts. McNair had been a NASA classmate (1978) of Bluford's.

The reaction was strong and swift. NASA suspended flights for more than two years while the agency investigated and regrouped. Even with her application on hold, the true risk of space travel clear as ever, and her own mother calling her, asking her if she would continue, Jemison was determined to see her plan through. The deaths were tragic, but the event to her was an accident, not a disaster. Space shuttles are full of explosive materials; it is not shocking that something bad could happen. "Accidents have happened and will happen," Jemison said in an interview. "But you don't stop getting into

The space shuttle *Challenger* launched on January 28, 1986.

cars just because there was an accident. You just have to figure out ways to make it safer." You also have to decide what you want more: to live in fear of a possible accident, or to take thoughtful risks and potentially reap serious rewards. Jemison was up for that challenge when, in June of 1987, she became one of fifteen people accepted into NASA out of a pool of more than two thousand applicants.

NASA Calls

The story of the minutes and hours immediately following Jemison's acceptance is a humorous one. NASA called her while she was in the middle of examining a patient. She received the amazing news of a lifetime, but she had to return to her patient and focus wholly on him! Sure enough, when she reentered the exam room, her mind was preoccupied. She couldn't stop thinking about how she was now an astronaut, and so her body took over. Acting automatically, she started performing a standard physical exam. The patient thought it all a little strange, especially since he had not come in not for a physical but for help with his back pain.

Jemison was told that she couldn't tell anyone the great news right away because NASA wanted to announce the crew at a noon press conference the next day. Jemison did divulge the news to her parents, who she knew would keep the secret, but she dutifully kept the information from everyone else. The next morning, her nurse stopped by her office to exclaim over her becoming an astronaut and tease her for not saying anything to him. Jemison checked her watch. It was still morning, so how did he know? For a brief moment she was worried, but she had been so careful not to say anything! The nurse went on to say that the office had been fielding phone calls from reporters all morning, and it dawned on her: NASA was on Eastern Time and she was in Los Angeles. The noon news had already been released.

Becoming a Role Model

Jemison said that when she applied to NASA, it didn't even cross her mind that she might become the first African American woman in space. "*I* wanted to go into space," she said, emphasizing that she as an individual, not a figurehead nor role model, had this goal. That was what mattered to her. "I couldn't have cared if there had been a thousand people in space before me or whether there had been none. I wanted to go."

That does not mean she ignored the history she was making once she was chosen for a flight. "The fact that I was the first woman of color in the world to go into space meant that I had a responsibility to use my perspective, my background, to bring a different set of possibilities to the equation," Jemison declared. She would show African American girls and women that they could be anyone, do anything, and go anywhere, and only the stars, literally, were the limits. She would also be an example for "older white males who sometimes make decisions on those careers of those little black girls," she told the Associated Press, as reported by the *New York Times* in 1992. True, long-lasting, sustainable change happens when all parties involved make new choices.

Candidate Training

Following a person's selection by NASA, the current procedure is that that person goes through a weeklong series of medical screenings and interviews. Anne McClain, one of the eight astronauts in NASA's class of 2013, shared with CBS News her experience with the interview process. She went through two rounds of interviews, the first in front of one hundred people and the second around fifty. It may sound terrifying, but they're just trying to get to know the applicant as an individual, not asking the applicant to "compute the escape velocity of a rocket or something like that, you know, in 20 seconds or less."

Those who pass that stage become official astronaut candidates and go through two years of training at the Johnson Space Center in Houston, Texas. McClain likened this to "being in grad school and boot camp at the same time." By the end, a candidate must be able to swim three pool lengths and tread water for ten minutes while wearing a flight suit and tennis shoes. Candidates are exposed to microgravity and periods of weightlessness up to forty times a day, as well as hyperbaric (high) and hypobaric (low) atmospheric pressure. They're also trained in the systems they'll encounter on the **International Space Station**, the activities and vehicles they may encounter outside the spaceship, and robots. Everyone takes Russian language classes because Russia is the other major player in space exploration.

Shuttle Crew

A spacecraft crew is made up of a commander, pilot, mission specialist, and payload specialist. The commander is in charge, with full responsibility for the vehicle and crew, making the ultimate call on matters pertaining to mission success and safety. The pilot assists in controlling and operating the vehicle as well as auxiliary mechanics, such as satellite retrieval systems.

Crewmembers have at least a bachelor's degree in engineering, biological or physical science, or math. Clinical or experimental psychology degrees are considered, but geography, nursing, and even aviation are not. Most astronauts have far more advanced degrees in their field, like doctorates, PhD or MD. NASA looks in detail at these degrees, and any average engineering degree is not enough. The astronaut has to have gone to a prestigious school, had remarkable teachers, or done exceptional work in his or her studies. Commanders and pilots also need to have at least one thousand hours piloting a jet aircraft. All astronauts who go into space should understand flight, but only those destined to sit behind the wheel of the spaceship have to be licensed pilots.

They must also be in peak physical condition, although, as of September 2007, NASA started to consider people who have had corrective vision surgery, such as LASIK. There's no age restriction; candidates have ranged from as young as twenty-six to as old as forty-six, with the average age of those applying being thirty-four years old. Additionally, they don't have to retire by a certain age. So far, practicing astronauts have been as old as fifty-six (Peggy Whitson) and seventy-seven (John Glenn) at launch. There is a set height requirement since living and working space is tight on a shuttle, and each ounce counts in a machine that needs to fly. Commanders and pilots need to be at least 5 feet 2 inches (1.57 m) and no more than 6 feet 3 inches (1.91 m).

Mission specialists, like Jemison, oversee onboard systems and experiments, among other tasks. They also are the astronauts who get to take spacewalks! They must meet similar requirements as those of commanders and pilots; they don't need flight experience but they need work and research experience. They can be 4 feet 10 inches (1.47 m) to 6 feet 4 inches (1.93 m) tall.

Payload specialists aren't NASA astronauts and may even be from a country other than the United States. They are included in a crew if they have specialized knowledge important to the specific mission.

The Parts of the Space Shuttle

A space shuttle is the whole spacecraft that launches from Earth. It is made up of three parts: the **orbiter**, where the crew lives and works; the external tank, which holds the bulk of the fuel; and two solid rocket boosters, which give the shuttle the oomph it needs during the first two minutes of takeoff.

It is the orbiter that actually bears what we think of as the shuttle's name. Since the orbiter can be reused, there have been only six in NASA history: the *Enterprise* (this was the test vehicle that was never used for an official flight), the *Columbia*, the *Challenger*, the *Discovery*, the *Atlantis*, and the *Endeavour*. An orbiter is a little over three school buses, lined up end to end, in length. The heaviest orbiter, the *Columbia*, weighed the equivalent of 13.4 African elephants.

The Mercury, Gemini, and Apollo programs, which each completed several missions, were NASA's first explorations into space, leading up to and including the moon landings. The manned shuttle program officially began in 1972, and each flight into space was called **STS** followed by a dash and a number, starting with STS-1 in 1981. The orbiters *Columbia*, *Challenger*, *Discovery*, *Atlantis*, and *Endeavour* flew many missions before NASA ended the program in 2011. NASA continues to operate, and one of its projects in development is the **SLS** (Space Launch System), based on the shuttle-derived rocket being designed to replace STS.

Jemison's Assignment

After her required on-site training at the Johnson Space Center, and while waiting for her name to be called for a NASA mission, Jemison worked as a technical liaison between the Johnson Space Center and the Kennedy Space Center in Cape Canaveral, Florida, monitoring shuttle and orbiter payloads and shuttle software. She eventually was assigned to the *Endeavour* as a science mission specialist to STS-47, an eight-day Spacelab Life Sciences cooperative mission between the United States and Japan. Mission specialists are the crew members allowed to walk in space and conduct experiments.

The History of Endeavour

On August 1, 1987, Congress granted permission for the construction of the *Endeavour* orbiter as one of the replacements for the *Challenger*. It arrived at the Kennedy Space Center Shuttle Landing Facility on May 7, 1991, transported by NASA's new shuttle carrier aircraft.

For the first time, an orbiter was named through a national competition. In May 1989, grade school and high school students chose to name the space shuttle after a ship that traveled the South Pacific in 1768. That *Endeavour* was captained by James Cook, who had been tasked by the British Admiralty and Royal Society to observe Venus over the island of Tahiti. This information would allow astronomers to calculate the distance between the sun and Earth. In addition to that, Cook and his crew of ninety-three, including eleven scientists and artists, charted New Zealand and Australia and survived traveling around the Great Barrier Reef. The artists sketched thousands of plant and animal specimens new to them, and the work of the scientists set a precedent for future voyages including scientists.

What Jemison Carried

Astronauts get to pack their own bags just like any traveler. In addition to clothes (such as one pair of underwear for every two days), they can bring personal items that collectively weigh under 2 pounds (0.9 kg) and can fit in a small box. If they're staying for a while at the International Space Station, they can receive care packages from home. The most common requests by astronauts are for chocolate, movies, and books.

When Jemison was packing for her historic flight, she thought carefully about what personal items she would bring. They should mean something to her, and they should say something to the world, since the media would report what she chose to bring. She said, "It was important to take to space with me things that represented people who sometimes are not included." There were no women and no people of color in the photos of the Apollo missions she otherwise so admired, and so she hadn't seen herself in them. Jemison knew she was not alone in feeling left out. Others "didn't see themselves, and so they didn't see the connection back to them." That connection among people is everything for Jemison. If a person doesn't see herself as an explorer or as part of the greater universe, so much of life will pass her by. Jemison upholds the belief that people will not work to change the world for the better if they don't see themselves as a part of it. "It's important that

Jemison gathers with the rest of the *Endeavour* crew for a shift-change meeting.

we start recognizing that every individual in society has skills and talents. Let them use those talents and not be so closed that we picture scientists and explorers and adventurers as one kind of stereotyped person," Jemison told her hometown paper, the *Chicago Tribune*, before her mission.

Her choices included an Alvin Ailey poster, and a bundu statue from the Sande, a secret women's society in West Africa, where Jemison did her Peace Corps service. In addition she brought a flag from an American women's society, Alpha Kappa Alpha, the oldest African American sorority, founded in 1908 at Howard University.

Sharon McDougle, Jemison's suit tech, later explained that, yes, it did mean something to her that a fellow African American woman would go into space. "I do feel it's more special to me when it's a black woman doing something for the first time ... That's my sister going into space."

The Launch

At 10:23 a.m. Eastern Daylight Time (EDT) on September 12, 1992, the *Endeavour* blasted off from Earth. It weighed 258,679 pounds (117,334.82 kg). It took about eight minutes from launch till orbit, about 191 miles (307 km) above the ground. During the last half of that ascent, Jemison said the pressure against her chest was intense, making her feel like she weighed three times as much as she did.

Even though she was aware of the risks of space travel and what a heavy responsibility she carried as one of the few people to ever go to space, Jemison said she wasn't afraid. She was excited and happy, achieving her goal after so many years of planning and working. Finally, she could see super clearly those stars she'd spent so many nights gazing at through her bedroom window. Through the shuttle's windows, the sky looks just as it does through bedroom windows on Earth, she later told Scholastic readers, except the stars are much brighter.

Work on the Endeavour

Aboard the *Endeavour* with Jemison were Commander Robert L. Gibson; Pilot Curtis L. Brown Jr.; fellow Mission Specialists Mark C. Lee, N. Jan Davis, and Jay Apt; and Payload Specialist Mamoru Mohri from Japan. Jemison worked blue shift, or night shift. Davis and Apt worked with her. The other three astronauts on the mission worked the day, or red, shift.

Jemison and her colleagues conducted more than forty-four experiments designed by American and Japanese scientists from those two countries' space agencies, universities, and corporations. Twenty-four experiments were in materials science and twenty in life sciences; Japan's space agency, NASDA, sponsored thirty-five of those, NASA sponsored seven, and they sponsored two together.

Materials science investigations covered such fields as biotechnology, electronic materials, fluid dynamics and transport phenomena, glasses and ceramics, metals and alloys, and acceleration measurements.

Life sciences included experiments on human health, cell separation and biology, developmental biology, animal and human physiology and behavior, space radiation, and biological rhythms. Jemison experimented on the crew to learn more about motion sickness in space. She tested both medicine and biofeedback as ways to prevent such sickness. When she learned biofeedback during training, she found it useful to her, but she couldn't be certain from her experiments on the *Endeavour*, limited by size of the test pool and length of time allowed, whether it could work for most people in most situations.

Jemison was coinvestigator on the bone cell research experiment conducted during the mission, learning more about what degree of bone loss occurs when humans spend time in outer space. She also considered frog egg fertilization and frog embryo development in space to learn about how reproduction is affected by the unique conditions found in space.

Jemison enjoyed her work because it was so creative. She has always loved dissecting problems, developing new solutions, and helping others understand.

Living in Space

Contrary to assumptions made popular through advertisements after the Apollo missions, Jemison and the crew did not only eat "astronaut food" products like Tang and space ice cream, typically a piece of ready-to-eat dehydrated or freeze-dried ice cream which almost feels like it "melts" in the mouth. Freeze drying is a process which uses low pressure to freeze and remove all of the moisture from a food. Astronauts do eat freeze-dried food, but usually they do so by mixing with water to rehydrate it back into recognizable meals. Everything from oatmeal and chili to shrimp cocktail and chicken à la king can be preserved in this way. They also carry food Jemison likened to canned goods, but in foil envelopes instead of aluminum cans. Heat and eat! Additionally, astronauts are allowed to bring "normal" food like chocolate, not specially preserved, just in the regular packaging.

A space shuttle toilet operates similar to one on an airplane, sucking the waste away with each flush. Liquid waste gets shot into space because it turns into ice there. The solid waste goes into a compacting container, which isn't emptied until the ship returns to the Kennedy Space Center.

Deconditioning is a problem for astronauts in space. Immediately upon leaving normal gravity, the body's muscles start weakening because there is no weight, and without resistance, not even the most minimal and accidental of weightlifting happens. Astronauts must exercise to keep their muscles strong. That includes the important heart muscle. In space, even it doesn't get worked the way it does on Earth; it doesn't pump blood at the same rate. Jemison said a popular exercise on the shuttle is riding stationary bikes.

Back on Earth

At 8:53:23 a.m. EDT on September 20, 1992, the space shuttled landed, weighing about 40,000 pounds (18,143 kg) less than it had when it took off. It had traveled 3.3 million miles (5.3 million km) in seven days, twenty-two hours, thirty minutes, and twenty-three seconds.

Being in space "made me feel very connected with the universe," Jamison said. "I felt my being was as much a part of this universe as any star, as any comet. It helped me to recognize that right now, we're in space. This Earth is part of this universe." The very first thing she saw when she looked out the spaceship window into space was the lights of Chicago, and it caused her to wonder what her younger self would think if she could meet her older self. "I think she would have been tickled."

Of course, her eight-year-old self also would have been irritated with what her adult self was tasked with as an astronaut.

Chicago, glowing far below her, was the first place Jemison saw when she looked out *Endeavour*'s window.

Young Jemison thought space exploration at the end of the century should have advanced to walking on Mars or circling Jupiter, not floating around just above Earth.

Life After NASA

Jemison would have liked to continue exploring space, but she also wants to push the boundaries of human knowledge and abilities. She wants everyone to be able to lend their unique talents in participation. She has said her motto is the single word "purpose." When asked by Scholastic readers if she'd accomplished all she wanted to do, having finally reached space and even made history doing so, she responded, "I certainly hope I haven't done everything I wanted to do in life! Otherwise, why would I still be here?" So it should not be surprising that she left NASA in March 1993, six months after her historic flight. She had discovered new goals to reach for. "The work that I do now," she said in that 2001 Scholastic interview, "really focuses on designing technology, so that as many people around this planet can share in our resources."

Empowering Others Around the World

She founded the Jemison Group to combine her interest in advancing technology with encouraging groups historically underrepresented in the sciences, such as women and racial minorities. Over the years, it's sponsored many projects, including Alafiya (meaning "good health" in the Yoruba language), which explores using satellite technology to help with health-care delivery in less accessible parts of the world. The Jemison Group has also supported companies such as BioSentient Corporation, a medical devices and services company focusing on physiological awareness to improve human performance.

This work led Dartmouth College to invite Jemison to teach environmental studies. Within this capacity, she taught sustainable development and technology design and ran the Jemison Institute for Advancing Technologies in Developing Countries. She has also been a visiting professor at Cornell University.

Biggest Challenge

Scholastic readers asked Jemison what her biggest challenge had been. That interview took place in 2001, long after Jemison's childhood in tumultuous 1960s Chicago, long after her years of study and service both in the United States and abroad, and long after her NASA career. She'd faced a lot of rough roads, but her answer to this question was this: "The biggest challenge we all face is to learn about ourselves and to understand our strengths and weaknesses."

She went on to say that we each need to accentuate our strengths as well as be mindful of our weaknesses. Those may need even more attention than our strengths because weaknesses are not so simply defined. They're not just the things we don't do well. They may also be our strengths out of control. A person might be "trying too hard. You might have to learn when to let go, or when to keep going," Jemison explained.

The key, Jemison said, "is to overcome the things in yourself that keep you from moving forward." That's important because when you know yourself and know how to manage yourself, then you can better respond to challenges that come from outside you. You may even be able to be proactive in situations rather than just reactive.

Inspiring the Next Generation

Under the Dorothy Jemison Foundation for Excellence, which Jemison founded in memory of her mother, The Earth We Share (TEWS) provides students ages twelve to sixteen from around the world with science education in a camp setting. Over four weeks each year, students participating in TEWS build critical-thinking and problem-solving skills in science settings. Science has a broad definition with varied practical applications to Jemison. She said the TEWS students "do things like predict the hot public stocks of the year 2030, and design the world's perfect house."

In October 2006, the Dorothy Jemison Foundation hosted the symposium Reality Leads Fantasy: Celebrating Women of Color in Flight. TEWS-Space Race launched in the summer of 2011 with a focus on Los Angeles–area students underserved and underrepresented in the sciences. It educates middle-school students and trains teachers.

Propelling Humanity into the Beyond

Jemison is the principal of 100 Year Starship, an initiative to ensure that within the next century all the capabilities exist to send humans to another star system, making use of human power across race, ethnicity, gender, geography, and discipline. As audacious a proposal as that is, Jemison has made it clear that inclusivity is the initiative's main focus. The program has been funded by the US Department of Defense's Defense Advanced Research Project Agency (DARPA). That said, Jemison explained, the initiative is not about war, and it's not really about meeting such a specific travel goal as reaching another star system in the next hundred years.

To reach far outer space would be cool, but it would be so difficult to accomplish, Jemison explained. We need new fuel technology and new life-support technology in order to do that. To explain, she suggested we imagine Los Angeles is Earth and New York City is Alpha Centauri, Earth's closest neighboring star. The *Voyager* spaceship has been traveling at 35,000 miles per hour (56,325 kmh) since 1977; on the Los Angeles–to–New York scale, it's gone only 1 mile (1.6 km). This means, with the technology we have today, it will take us seventy thousand years to reach Alpha Centauri. That said, one of the initiatives of 100 Year Starship has been working on building an actual starship through intense workshops, and the group held a big public symposium in Silicon Valley in October 2015. In August 2016, NASA itself announced a Mars program, funded by public and private money and spearheaded by six companies in addition to NASA. The group has two years to develop concept studies.

We need to be able to travel faster to have any hope of reaching somewhere far away within the span of a human life. We can't use chemical rockets; we need to be able to use fission and fusion, and generate and store that energy. Even if we could vastly increase our speed and cut our travel time to fifty years, we'd still have to figure out closed environmental life support systems. At that speed, you can't stop for supplies. You have to pack everything you will need for your entire multiyear journey on the ship.

So the mission of 100 Year Starship is really about "fostering those radical leaps in knowledge and technology design and human systems that happen when you take on a really, really tough problem," according to Jemison. Solving these issues, like those of sustainability, will help us here and now on Earth.

Educational Impact and Distinctions

Jemison has been a member of several major medical and scientific organizations, including the American Medical Association, the American Chemical Society, and the American Association for the Advancement of Science. She served on the board of directors of the World Sickle Cell Foundation from 1990 to 1992. She has also served as an advisory committee member of the American Express Geography Competition and an honorary board member of the Center for the Prevention of Childhood Malnutrition.

She's been the *Essence* Science and Technology Award winner and the Gamma Sigma Woman of the Year. She won the *Ebony* Black Achievement Award and has been inducted into the National Women's Hall of Fame and National Medical Association Hall of Fame. The Mae C. Jemison Academy in Detroit, Michigan, was named in her honor because it focused on teaching preschoolers through second graders math and science. Though now closed, the academy was a school of choice within the Detroit Public Schools system, receiving national recognition for its pioneering curriculum. Wilbur Wright Junior College in Chicago also named an institution after her, the Mae C. Jemison Science and Space Museum.

Jemison launched the University of Virginia's School of Engineering and Applied Science's yearlong (2016–2017) Excellence Through Diversity Distinguished Learning Series. The series is one of the first initiatives of the department's new associate dean for diversity and engagement, John Fitzgerald Gates, who was hired specifically to redefine diversity as "excellence expressing itself through the intersection of perspectives and lived experiences," rather than continue to

Where No One
Has Gone Before

Just as humans have long dreamed of flying in general, we have for a very long time wished we could fly past Earth's atmosphere and into space. Technology had to catch up to our imaginations before space travel could happen, and it did so in a rush in the early twentieth century. Airplanes became feasible for human transport in 1903, with the Wright brothers' first successful flight. After that, further airplane and military advancements led to humanity reaching the stars.

China has for centuries shot off rockets, but they became useful for more than short-range military and ceremony purposes only about one hundred years ago. Nazi Germany attacked London with V-2 missiles, which demonstrated distance, height, and speed capabilities previously unheard of: they traveled across 200 miles (322 km), arched to a peak of 60 miles (97 km), and moved at 3,500 miles per hour (5,633 kmh).

After World War II, the United States and the Soviet Union (USSR) started developing missile programs. For many years during the space race, the two countries ping-ponged with firsts in space exploration. On October 4, 1957, the USSR launched an unmanned satellite. On January 31, 1958, the United States' first satellite orbited Earth.

In 1961, the first ship safely sent a human into space and into an orbit around Earth. This was *Vostok 1*, built by Sergei Korolev's Soviet team and piloted by Yuri Gagarin. Later that same year, American Alan Shepard went into space. The

In 1958, the full-size model of the first American satellite, *Explorer 1*, was revealed.

following year, John Glenn became the first American to orbit Earth. Neil Armstrong, an American, became the first human to set foot on the moon, on July 20, 1969.

In the 1990s, during the Gulf War, aerospace technology again held a key place in military situations: the United States and its allies were able to use their satellites to their advantage. From the highest point possible, outer space, they monitored enemy troops, which allowed them to see attacks in the planning stages. They also navigated their own forces more precisely than they could have with only ground navigation, since what few features there were in the desert battlefields could shift with the winds.

First Lady Michelle Obama invited Jemison to speak at
Woodrow Wilson High School in Washington, DC, in 2009.

focus only on proportional representation of racial minorities and women in engineering.

Her Experiments Continue

In late 2016, Jemison became a national advocate for Bayer Corporation's Making Science Make Sense program. Its goal is to provide students across the country with one million hands-on science experiments by 2020. Through these, a student might learn how science plays a role in nearly every field in life. Even hair stylists use science: "When we go to the hairdresser, we want her to know something about pH balance," Jemison said, since an off pH balance causes hair to become brittle and prone to breakage.

A study the company conducted confirmed what Jemison has known: there's a severe disconnect between science perception and science education. In the study, 99 percent of teachers called science "exciting, creative and interesting," but only 42 percent used those words to describe how it's taught in schools. Young people will continue to feel a disconnect between life and science if science continues to seem like something that has no purpose in day-to-day life.

Jemison thinks the journey is as important as the destination when it comes to science, sometimes even more important. "A big part of engaging kids in science is not getting the single, correct answer. It's being willing to work with students to discover the correct answer."

Sixty and Not Stopping

In her sixties, Jemison is both coming full circle and shooting for the stars. In 2016, she returned to the state of her birth,

Alabama, to cut the ribbon for a new school that bears her name. Jemison High School in Huntsville is high tech, with courses in cyber security and a 3D titanium printer for the students to use, and high profile in more than just its name. "My pledge," Jemison said at the opening ceremony, is "to help in any way I can … because you can't just come to a school named for you, show up at the ribbon cutting and walk away."

As grounded as Jemison is, she continues to dream. While supporting Bayer Corporation's Making Science Make Sense program is her primary side work, her main job is leading 100 Year Starship. If humans do reach for Mars in her lifetime, she says she'd take the opportunity to go "in a heartbeat."

Jemison is active on Twitter (@maejemison), and her tweets reflect the engaged person she is. She hash-tagged her tweet about the 2016 anniversary of her flight to space with #DaringMakesADifference and repeated that hashtag when she celebrated Jeanette Epps's assignment to the International Space Station, announced in January 2017. As the first African American ISS crew member, Epps surely takes inspiration from Jemison. In addition, Jemison tweets about her many presentations and talks, Making Science Make Sense, 100 Year Starship, *Star Trek*, and on brilliant people such as Neil deGrasse Tyson. She honored John Glenn when he died in December 2016 and cheered Katherine Johnson when she turned ninety-eight in August 2016. She also tweets about things unrelated to space, offering her support to Hillary Clinton in the 2016 presidential election, mourning the death of journalist and African American pioneer Gwen Ifill in November 2016, recommending a movie about girls and chess *(Queen of Katwe)*, and agreeing with fashion consultant Tim Gunn on how maddening it is that designers don't seem to want to dress the average American woman. She retweeted about the discovery of the first known bit of fossilized dinosaur brain, in October 2016, and exchanged *Star Trek* pleasantries on her 2016 birthday with the @emotuvok account. "Yo people!" her 2017 New Year's Day tweet began. "2017 is here! Let's make ourselves proud!!!!"

Jemison is also a cat lover. Some even acted as uninvited lab assistants during her childhood home experimentation. As of 2006, she had four cats, Dallas, Sapphire, Nathan, and LeShawn.

four

Inspirations and Challenges

"Every individual in society has skills and talents. Let them use those talents and not be so closed that we picture scientists and explorers and adventurers as one kind of stereotyped person." —Mae C. Jemison

Jemison is all about the loop of inspiration: tying those who came before with those acting now for the benefit of those who will come next. Or perhaps a better word than "loop" is "web": threads of people doing their best and influencing each other in the process, branching in all directions and connecting with one another at a variety of points.

Opposite: Jemison, a popular and inspiring figure, spoke at the 2016 Forbes Women's Summit in New York City.

Challenge is of lesser use to Jemison; if it must be referenced, she finds in that word not adversity but a call to action.

Inspirations

Jemison has said that she admires many people. Some have directly mentored and advocated for her; some have never met her but have encouraged her by example. As her primary motivators, she names her parents, as they were her mentors and were steadfast supporters of her vision. They always treated her as a fully capable human who mattered, and they made her confident that her abilities were equal to anyone else's. As Jemison said, "I was the ultimate women's libber when I was a little girl."

Dorothy Green and Charlie Jemison

All three of the Jemison children were taught by their parents to value education and, because the world was so vast, "to be at least good in a number of" things, Jemison remembered in her father's 2004 *Chicago Tribune* obituary. She obviously valued their advice, as did her sister and brother. Ada became a child psychiatrist and served as medical director of a program at a hospital, and Charles became a real estate broker. For his father's obituary, the younger Charles said, "One of the things he told me when I was a teenager [was] I had to go to college even if it was just for a day."

Through word and deed during her twenty-five-year career as an educator in Chicago public schools, Jemison's mother demonstrated to her students, their parents, other teachers, and her own children, her belief "that each person can and should be expected to achieve a level of excellence that allows a unique contribution to society." This quote can be found on the website for the foundation Jemison set up in her mother's name. Just as important, each person has the responsibility to support those around them. This means everyone is excelling, being supported, and giving support. This global web of shared concern has inspired Jemison's work in schools and tech companies.

As a kid, Jemison thought it was "really cool" that her mother worked. Women working outside the home was less common then than it is now. According to the US census, there were 9.8 million stay-at-home moms in 1969 and 5.7 million in 2009. In 1969, 44 percent of married women with children under fifteen years of age did not work outside the home; that number had dropped to 26 percent in 2009. The numbers are not easily understood. For example, African American women have always worked in greater numbers than white women. The fact that the Census Bureau has changed its racial terms over the decades muddles those numbers, but popular perception has been that women didn't have careers the way men did, and that, at least, makes Jemison's childhood approval of her mother's career interesting. She recognized from a young age that it was good for women to work, even when others may have thought it unusual.

Just as seemingly unusual as a woman working outside the home was a man working within it, but Jemison's father taught her that was good, too. He was a "man's man," Jemison said for his obituary, but that didn't lead him to scoff at domestic work. "He would also braid my hair for kindergarten," she said. He tended the gardens at their homes, was a good cook, and was happy to be in charge of meals while his wife was working outside the home. Jemison's father taught her that she had a voice that mattered. She hung out with his friends and him, even playing cards (and learning to count cards!) with them when she was six or seven years old. Speaking of her time with these adults, she later said, "[They] thought it was really cool, my assertiveness. Never was I not allowed to be in the conversation. Never was I put out of the political discussions."

Jemison had her parents' support throughout her education, travel adventures, and career firsts. They helped with whatever she wanted to do in school projects and extracurricular activities. She said, "They would find the money, time, and energy to help me be involved." They, along with her uncle and other adults in her life, took her to Chicago's Museum of Science and Industry, the Field Museum of natural history, and the Brookfield Zoo, from which she learned more about the world around her and a wide range of careers in the sciences. Some of her teachers gave her room to develop self-study programs—"let me go off and do things, explore on my own"—and some recognized her intelligence and offered her advanced study. "One math teacher," she said, "took me and another student aside during our senior year and taught us solid analytic geometry." As important, her parents showed her every day how to be a scientist. "My parents were the best scientists I knew, because they were always asking questions," she maintained.

Carol Espy-Wilson

Sometimes a person's most important mentors are people at the same level. We can learn a lot from the people who are learning right alongside us. Jemison has named her Stanford classmate Carol Espy-Wilson, the first African American woman to earn a doctorate in electrical engineering from Massachusetts Institute of Technology (MIT), as someone she admires.

Using an interdisciplinary approach (as Jemison also likes to do), drawing from the fields of engineering, linguistics, and speech science, Espy-Wilson founded OmniSpeech, which works to improve poor cell-phone sound quality in parts of the world where inexpensive phones are prevalent. This work could be extrapolated to better all communication devices, including hearing aids.

Kindred Spirits

In her testimony before the Senate on the fortieth anniversary of Title IX, Jemison named Sally Ride, Kathryn Sullivan, and Eileen Collins as her kindred spirits. They all grew up at a time when women and racial minorities were not astronauts, yet they all inspired each other—and millions around the world—with their eventual space feats.

Sally Ride: First American Woman in Space

There are many similar threads through Sally Ride's and Jemison's careers and beliefs about their roles as aerospace pioneers. Ride launched American society another few paces forward on June 18, 1983, when she became the first American woman in space. Russia, the other great leader in space exploration, sent its first woman into space twenty years and two days before the United States did. Valentina Tereshkova spent almost three days in space after leaving Earth's atmosphere on June 16, 1963. There seemed to be no good reason why the United States would continue to prevent

American women from going up, yet NASA remained set in its decision.

When Ride was selected for a mission five years after women were finally allowed to join NASA (she and five other women had been in that graduating class), she changed the way Americans viewed space politics. "The fact that I was going to be the first American woman to go into space carried huge expectations along with it," Ride said in an interview for the twenty-fifth anniversary of her flight, as reported by NASA. She also said that emotions and busyness on the day of that launch kept her from focusing on the responsibility: "I didn't really think about it that much at the time—but I came to appreciate what an honor it was to be selected to be the first to get a chance to go into space."

Near the twentieth anniversary of her own historic mission, Jemison said something similar about her experiences, in testimony before the United States Senate Committee on Health, Education, Labor and Pensions: "I felt a strong, special responsibility to fly this mission on behalf of those who had come before me and who, because of gender or race, had been denied the opportunity I … now had. And I was also aware that in many ways I was making this flight on behalf of others who would come after me." Jemison has spoken often of how important it is for people to see others who look like them represented in various careers.

Indeed, Gloria Steinem, *Ms.* magazine editor, in 1983 said of Ride's flight, "Millions of little girls are going to sit by their television sets and see they can be astronauts, heroes, explorers and scientists." From the time Ride left NASA in 1989 to her death in 2012, she dedicated her career to education, including starting the company Sally Ride Science in 2001 to encourage girls and young women to pursue careers in science, technology, engineering, and math.

Kathryn Sullivan: First American Woman to Spacewalk

A year after Ride's first flight, it was her NASA classmate Kathryn Sullivan's turn to make history. She became the first American woman to step outside her space shuttle and "walk" in outer space. Sullivan floated in space for three and a half hours, tethered to a ship that was traveling 17,500 miles per hour (28,160 kmh) about 140 miles (225 km) above Earth.

This also meant this was the first time a woman had worn an Extravehicular Mobility Unit (EMU), the big white spacesuit. These suits were pieced together with premade arm, leg, and torso units. Because you could mix and match these parts, each suit fit its wearer fairly well, but it wasn't the same as a custom-made suit. Sullivan reported that her suit was comfortable, though her elbows and knees didn't quite align with the corresponding joints in the arm and leg units.

This "space sailor" took the Greek root of her "astronaut" title literally after leaving NASA in 1993, immediately accepting an appointment by the president to be chief scientist of the National Oceanic and Atmospheric Administration (NOAA). Later, in 2014, she received Senate confirmation to serve as the under secretary of commerce for oceans and atmosphere and NOAA administrator.

Eileen Collins: First Female Shuttle Pilot

Eileen Collins was a contemporary of Jemison's. They were born almost exactly one month apart, Jemison on October 17, 1956, and Collins November 19, 1956. They graduated from college one year apart: Jemison in 1977 in California, Collins in 1978, across the country, from Syracuse University in New York. Collins joined NASA as an astronaut in 1990, two years before Jemison took her historic flight. Collins was a part of a number of important milestones, Her pilot training course at Oklahoma's Vance Air Force Base was one of the first to include women; Collins graduated from it in 1978. When she graduated from the Air Force Test Pilot School at Edwards Air Force Base in 1990, she was only the second woman to have done so.

Five years later, in February 1995, Collins became the first female astronaut to pilot a mission. She guided the *Discovery* to its rendezvous with the Russian space station Mir. She took time off to have a child but didn't lose her place in the system for this decision. By May 1997, she was piloting her second mission, on the *Atlantis*, and on July 23, 1999, she commanded her first mission, assuming the highest place of power a female astronaut had ever occupied.

Encouraging Forces

Encouragement doesn't have to come directly addressed to you. Look for guidance even from people who will never meet you. Jemison does. She said former US president Jimmy Carter's work has encouraged her, just by example, over the years. She appreciated his vision as president, like when he formally stood against neutron bombs, and admires the decades of work he's accomplished as a private citizen, much of which has focused on people in developing countries getting "a fair stake" in global resources. Many other people and organizations offer support as well.

WASP, Women Airforce Service Pilots

The web page for Jemison's Reality Leads Fantasy—Celebrating Women of Color in Flight demands greater recognition for the women of color in whose footsteps women of today, including Jemison, have walked. These include members of the WASP, Women Airforce Service Pilots, women who flew for the American military decades before they'd be officially allowed into service.

While NASA didn't accept female astronaut candidates till 1978, the US Army Air Forces (USAAF) accepted their abilities all the way back in 1944, at least in word if not in deed. "It is on the record that women can fly as well as men," said Henry "Hap" Arnold, the commanding general of the USAAF. He

Jacqueline Cochran (*center*) directed the Women Airforce Service Pilots and supervised the training of female pilots.

proclaimed this at the end of a two-year experiment, 1942 to 1944, that trained more than 1,100 female civilian volunteers to fly military aircraft, including bombers. World War II was raging; all available male pilots were needed overseas, flying combat missions. To fill the gaps, the military trained women to fly noncombat missions, and women expected to then be allowed into the military. Instead, women weren't accepted until the 1970s. Even those in WASP weren't granted official honors until 2010, when they were awarded the US Congress's highest civilian honor, the Congressional Gold Medal.

National Public Radio reported on the awarding of the medal with a story about one of the WASP, Margaret Phelan Taylor. *Life* magazine had published a cover story about WASP in 1943, and nineteen-year-old Taylor decided she wanted in. Her dad loaned her $500 for a pilot's license. Now she had everything she needed for joining WASP—except for height. She was 0.5 inches (1.3 centimeters) shorter than the requirement. When she arrived at the WASP training base, Avenger Field in Sweetwater, Texas, and met the other petite recruits, she realized she was not the only one who had stood on her toes to sneak by the requirement.

The head of the program, Jacqueline Cochran, was an expert pilot herself; she would, a few years later, be the first woman to break the sound barrier. Under her guidance, the WASP achieved safety records as good as or better than the records of their male counterparts. That was especially impressive considering the conditions the WASP flew in. Flying is dangerous enough, but flying as a woman in what was at the time a man's world carried extra concerns. For one, the parachutes the pilots were to use if they needed to bail on a failing airplane were too big for the female frame. It forced the women into terrible decisions. Taylor was ferrying a plane across the country when she saw smoke in the cockpit. She was over the vast desert of Arizona and California, and she had to think, "I'm not going until I see flame." Neither facing a fire nor jumping possibly without a parachute was ideal, so she had to push both options to their extreme moment.

Reality Leads Fantasy highlighted WASP Hazel Lee, a Chinese American woman born in Portland, Oregon, in 1912, as a woman Jemison is encouraged by. At the time that Lee earned her pilot's license, less than 1 percent of American pilots were women. In a sad twist, she was in China during the early days of World War II, and that country wouldn't accept her help flying planes, even though the Chinese military was desperate for pilots to fly against Japan. She returned to the United States and passed the WASP training, but again, she wasn't allowed fully into a military in desperate need of people power. Still, she died in service to her country, in a midair collision with another plane while she ferried a fighter plane from New York to Montana.

WISP, Woman in Space Program

As young Jemison was assuring her kindergarten teacher that she would be a scientist when she grew up, thirteen women were participating in their own experiment that would help Jemison realize her future. NASA and the Ninety-Nines, an organization of female aviators, discuss these women of WISP on their websites, and Jemison herself referenced their impact in her 2012 testimony before the United States Senate Committee on Health, Education, Labor and Pensions. In that speech, which celebrated the fortieth anniversary of Title IX, Jemison described WISP as "perhaps a forgotten chapter in

Wally Funk, Rhea Hurrle, and Jerrie Cobb (*from left to right*) of the Mercury Thirteen

the history of American Space Exploration … a chapter that might have been written quite differently had Title IX come into effect far earlier than it did."

The program was known as the Fellow Lady Astronaut Trainees (FLATs), Woman in Space Program (WISP), or the Mercury Thirteen, and sounds very much like a NASA program, but it wasn't. It ran from 1960 to 1961, and NASA wasn't recruiting, training, or at all considering female astronauts in 1960. It was, however, a program that mimicked NASA's programming in many ways. In some ways, it even surpassed the world leader.

William Randolph "Randy" Lovelace II and Brigadier General Donald Flickinger had worked with the astronauts of NASA's Mercury program (which sent the first American man into space). From that, their curiosity blossomed, leading them to ask: What about female astronauts? Their interest was based in practicality. Women were usually smaller and lighter than men, so, it was thought, they may fare better in the cramped quarters of spacecraft. Their size also meant they used less oxygen than men, useful in a place without naturally occurring oxygen. Heart attacks struck men more than women, so the scientists surmised that women would have more of a chance of surviving the unknown effects of microgravity on the cardiovascular system.

They even assumed that women's reproductive systems would be less affected by radiation then men's. Still, as the *New York Times* wrote in its 2012 obituary for Sally Ride, of the five crew members of her 1983 *Challenger* flight, it was she, the only female in the group, who received questions about spaceflight affecting her reproductive organs. Jacqueline Cochran, who had headed World War II's WASP and was also

Lovelace's friend, eventually joined to advise the women of WISP, and she paid the women's testing expenses.

Progress usually happens not with sweeping change by organizations but with first steps taken by a few individuals—and then a few more people take those steps, and then more, and only then is there institutional and systemic change. That was what happened here too: these scientists so believed that women might be just as effective in space as men that they took the risk to perform these experiments. Lovelace would say at the Space and Naval Medicine Congress in Sweden in 1960 that "there is no question but that women will eventually participate in space flight."

WISP Testing

The privately held Lovelace Foundation for Medical Education and Research had developed the physical tests for the Mercury astronauts, and Lovelace was also head of NASA's Special Committee on Bioastronautics. The group therefore decided to start by putting women through the physical paces of the men. The woman they started with was Geraldyn "Jerrie" Cobb, who'd already made a name for herself in the flying community.

Cobb passed easily, and after this success, the program was opened to more women. More than seven hundred women applied, but only those with at least one thousand flight hours were considered. Many had logged way more hours than the men selected for Mercury. For example, at ten thousand flight hours, Cobb had double what John Glenn, the most experienced pilot in the men's Mercury group, had. Ultimately, nineteen women were tested, and thirteen, or 68 percent, passed. This was a stronger ratio than the men's group, of whom only eighteen of thirty-two passed (56 percent). The men involved admitted the women's excellence: Donald Kilgore, a doctor who examined both the women and the men, said, "They were all extraordinary women and outstanding pilots and great candidates for what was proposed. They came out better than the men in many categories." Lovelace agreed: "Certain qualities of the female space pilot are preferable to those of her male colleague."

According to the Ninety-Nines, the testing, for men and women, took place over three phases:

In phase one, the candidates participated in a series of eighty-seven tests. Among them was a stomach test, which involved the candidate swallowing 3 feet (0.9 m) of rubber hose, and a brain wave test, which required eighteen needles stuck into the head. During this phase, each candidate drank a pint of radioactive water.

Phase two consisted of psychological and psychiatric testing. The isolation tank test was one of the most intense of these because it rendered useless all five senses. The participant was in a circular 8-foot- (2.4 m) deep tank of body-temperature water in a small, dark room without air circulation or humidity. The pool and room were vibration-proofed. There was nothing, really, to see, hear, touch, taste, or smell. Within six hours under such sensory deprivation conditions, the subconscious mind will take over, causing the person to hallucinate. Cobb spent more than nine hours in the tank. Wally Funk, another candidate, took the record, with ten hours thirty-five minutes in the tank, although the Ninety-Nines' website reports that she admitted to taking "breaks" by napping.

Phase three happened at different test sites. The participants traveled, for example, to the El Toro Marine Corps Base to undergo a high-altitude-chamber test and the Martin-Baker

Two Women on the *Endeavour*

Nancy Jan Davis was the one other female astronaut on Jemison's history-making 1992 flight. Born three years before Jemison, Davis was very much her contemporary. As two women in a career dominated by men, the two surely influenced each other. As a white person, she didn't face racial discrimination as Jemison did, but Davis had to work hard to overcome restrictions based on her gender. She also faced another layer of discrimination: NASA's policy against married astronauts flying together. Davis's partner was another astronaut.

Born in Cocoa Beach, Florida, Davis grew up in Huntsville, Alabama, nicknamed Rocket City because of all the space-exploration work done there. Growing up in the space-crazy era of the 1960s and the space-focused city of Huntsville, Davis was excited about space travel, but she didn't think she would ever work in space because she was a girl. Regardless, she was interested in science and earned degrees in applied biology and mechanical engineering. This did in fact lead to a job as an aerospace engineer at NASA, specifically the Marshall Space Flight Center. When the first female astronaut candidates were accepted in 1978, Davis was in a perfect position to reconsider her career.

Once women were allowed in the space program, NASA became worried about fraternization between astronauts on missions and banned married couples from going into space on the same mission. Davis and Mark Lee were both selected for the space shuttle *Endeavour* (STS-47) flight in 1992. They

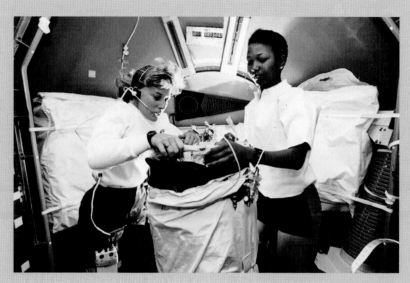

N. Jan Davis and Mae Jemison worked alongside each other during their *Endeavour* mission in space.

secretly married beforehand and revealed what they had done to NASA only once it was too late to train alternate astronauts. They were allowed to fly together, and NASA has since changed its policy about couples. No other spouses have flown together since Davis and Lee, however.

seat-ejection test. The centrifuge test simulated the gravitational forces present during lift-off and reentry.

The book *Almost Astronauts: 13 Women Who Dared to Dream* notes some of the other tests: For one test, researchers asked the participants 195 questions designed to annoy or anger. In another, participants were strapped on tilt tables and rocked wildly, blood pressure and heart rate measured every few minutes. In a third, a researcher injected freezing-cold water into each participant's ears. A frozen inner ear bone induces vertigo, something pilots can experience that is very dangerous, since it causes disorientation and imbalance. Cobb reported that when the water hit her inner ear, her hand involuntarily fell from the chair arm, and she couldn't move it back. Her vision spun, and she was in pain. The researchers just waited her vertigo out, timing how long it lasted.

In 1962, the group was scheduled to travel to the Naval School of Aviation Medicine in Florida to be tested on military equipment and planes. Two of the women quit their jobs to do this. Mere days before they were to be there, the navy called it off. Without an official request from NASA, which the agency would not give, the military would not grant use of their facilities.

WISP Lobbying

Cobb and WISP Jane Hart, whose husband was a US senator, lobbied President Kennedy and Vice President Lyndon Johnson. They weren't greeted by friendly faces. Cobb said Johnson told her, "Jerrie, if we let you or other women into the space program, we have to let blacks in, we'd have to let Mexican-Americans in, we have to let every minority in and we just can't do it."

Despite that, in July of that year, Representative Victor Anfuso, a Republican from New York, convened hearings before a subcommittee of the House Committee on Science and Astronautics. These hearings are a somewhat overlooked step in the fight for equality in the workplace, occurring two years before the 1964 Civil Rights Act made sex discrimination illegal. It was all moot, since no woman at that time could meet NASA's requirement that all astronauts be military jet pilots. The program was over without warning. Although nothing had actually changed, the sexism of the country's leadership became starkly apparent.

The United States was in the middle of the Cold War with the Soviet Union. The two countries hated and feared each other. Ugly propaganda came from both sides. So when the USSR's Valentina Tereshkova became the first female in space the very year after NASA refused to alter its rules for any one of the thirteen qualified women waiting for a chance, there should have been embarrassed, frustrated outrage from Americans. Cobb certainly was upset, expressing sadness that a woman seemingly less qualified than her and her colleagues (Tereshkova wasn't a pilot but an amateur parachutist) had gone first. Clare Boothe Luce, who had criticized NASA, the American government, and the American public in an article in *Life* magazine soon after the 1962 congressional hearing, wrote a follow-up piece pointing out that America had no good excuse for missing this opportunity.

Resistance

As an African American woman who spoke her mind in the twentieth century, Jemison had a lot of people working against her success. Some people directly hated her or actively tried to prevent her from advancing in her education and career.

Sometimes the Scariest Things Are Those We Know

"My baby's on top of an inferno," Jemison's mother exclaimed as she watched the *Endeavour* launch on September 12, 1992. Space travel is risky. The shuttle is full of dangerous materials and travels at incredible speeds into space void of oxygen. Fortunately, Jemison never experienced serious mishaps during her time in space. As a black woman in a discriminatory society, she faced her biggest risks on Earth.

One of the scariest incidents happened when she was nearly twelve years old in Chicago. That year, 1968, was tumultuous across the country. Martin Luther King Jr. was assassinated in April in Memphis, Tennessee, and in August, the Democratic National Convention was held in Jemison's hometown. Jemison watched the National Guard, called in by the Chicago's mayor to oppose civil rights protestors, march through her own neighborhood. "I remember being afraid for my father going to work that day," she said in a speech at Clemson University in 2016. She pushed through her feelings of fear and anger: "I reminded myself that I was as much a part of this United States as the Guardsmen," she told Scholastic in 2001.

In that same interview, Jemison offered advice to young women: "Understand that sometimes other people won't have the same vision of you that you have of yourself. Don't accept other people's limitations as being reality. Also, understand that you have as much right as anyone else to be in this world, and to be in any profession you want. That's the most important

Protests on issues like racism, sexism, and the Vietnam War caused unrest in many cities, including Chicago.

thing—you don't have to wait for permission." She had every right to occupy the same space as law enforcement, and all of us have every right to occupy space in school, work, and other sectors of life. When Jemison was a girl and young woman in the 1960s and 1970s, it was going against the norm to believe as she did. It still is, in many instances, today.

Some people worked against her by trying to downplay or excuse those racist and sexist words and actions. She has said that she remembers being "really, really irritated" that there were no women astronauts in the Apollo program. She added, "I remember people trying to explain to me why there weren't." Not only did she see racism and sexism before her but she had to deal with the voices of others who tried to tell her she had to just accept bigotry.

Even after she went to space and returned a hero, Jemison was met with ugly attitudes. The principal at an elementary school she visited told her to her face that he asked only his male teachers to share information about Space Camp with students since men are more knowledgeable than women in science.

Of course, one of the most prominent and problematic oppositions to the success of Jemison and other women and people of color striving to be astronauts was the thing closest to them: NASA. Without that agency, they wouldn't be astronauts—couldn't be astronauts—yet the agency tried so hard for so many years to prevent them from being even considered for the job. At her address in the Extraordinary Women lecture series, Jemison said that even though women were testing better than men in the physical exams, even though "women were originally thought by many doctors to make better astronauts," when NASA removed gender and race restrictions, still "the first people they chose were men."

Fortunately, Jemison has never believed any of this opposition. She's mindful of preconceived notions by others, and how they might affect her and others, but she has no time for the "'woe is me' stuff." She has walked her chosen career path to help "determine the future" of engineering and space.

Part of how she does this is by reminding girls and young women that they are allowed to make decisions. They can empower themselves by doing three things, in Jemison's opinion: First, understand that they have the right to be involved. Second, know that they have something important to contribute. Third, decide that they will take the risk to contribute what they can.

five

The Future of Space

"The sociocultural, political, scientific, and technical communities must see human travel to the stars as not just aspirational for a few, but necessary for life here on Earth to prosper and reach its full potential." —Mae C. Jemison

J emison has said that her life's motto is "purpose." It seems she puts that intention toward bringing a diverse group of people together and the mission of working to find multidisciplinary solutions to our world's issues. Some of her direct actions have been discussed in earlier chapters; the following are ways the fields she's worked in are growing from what was, and making strides toward the future.

Opposite: Jemison is a lead supporter of Bayer's Making Science Make Sense program encouraging children in science.

Charles Frank Bolden

Jemison has always emphasized that while she was the first African American woman in space, she wasn't the first African American in space. She wasn't even the only African American in the program at that time. There were five other working African American astronauts then. Her feats are theirs, and to some degree, she is but one brick in the foundation that people today are building on.

A one-mission astronaut like Jemison didn't directly get Charles Frank Bolden his job as NASA's twelfth administrator, becoming the first African American to lead the agency. Yet without Jemison's pioneering acts, the past would not have been as strong as it is to support President Barack Obama's decision to appoint Bolden.

Bolden led NASA from July 17, 2009, until January 12, 2017. Earlier in his career with NASA, he went into space four times, twice as a pilot and twice as a commander. His professional life started with an education in the Naval Academy and then flying more than one hundred combat missions as a pilot with the US Marine Corps. He almost didn't get into the academy—none of his South Carolina representatives or senators would nominate him because of his race. Senator Strom Thurmond sharply rejected him. Then, after every career milestone, Bolden "got a handwritten note from him, you know, saying congratulations," Bolden said in an interview with National Public Radio in 2016.

Inspiring Others

Without a doubt Jemison, has been an inspiration to countless of people. Some individuals have gone on to be inspirations themselves, and some have named Jemison as a direct influence on their lives.

Sharon McDougle

Sharon McDougle was Jemison's spacesuit tech before Jemison's September 12, 1992, launch into space. Astronauts can dress themselves—they must when they're in outer space—but help whenever possible lessens the stress. Also, during trainings, suit techs are needed to help size the suit and improve upon its fit.

Before NASA, McDougle had been an aerospace physiology technician with the Air Force. The SR-71 and U-2 reconnaissance aircraft crew members she worked with wore the same type of pressure suit that astronauts wore. They of course never left Earth's atmosphere, but they flew high enough and fast enough that they needed special suits. This

Sharon McDougle looks serious as she concentrates on fitting Jemison in her spacesuit, but she's as excited as Jemison is.

prepared McDougle for her work with NASA; however, nothing had prepared her emotionally to be Jemison's suit tech. She said that was the flight she would "cherish the most."

As soon as McDougle heard that Jemison was on the flight manifest, she knew she wanted to be her suit tech. The board listing crew names went up in the tech lab, and McDougle immediately put her name by Jemison's. McDougle was "proud," she said in an interview with the NASA Johnson Space Center Oral History Project, to be the only African American woman in her department, and she wanted to help the first African American woman into space. It was a "kinship, that family feeling" she felt, even though Jemison and McDougle didn't meet until they worked together.

Their first meeting was a fit check, when McDougle determined everything from Jemison's diaper size to harness size. She was like a tailor, measuring everything to make a perfect fit. She said it can be tricky to fit a woman because suits were patterned for the male form, so even the narrowest of female hips and smallest of breasts can still affect the sizing. The final fit check is two days before launch. Between those checks, astronauts wear their suits to a variety of training sessions, so techs help with those times, too. If a suit is going to be worn, the assigned tech is there. The day of the launch, the tech performs an unpressurized and pressurized leak check before the astronaut is strapped in; once the astronaut is fastened into the orbiter, the tech inflates the suit one more time, just in case something happened on the way to the shuttle.

McDougle admires Jemison for her intelligence and bravery as well as her personality and heart. "She's in a league of her own," McDougle said. She hadn't realized how extensive Jemison's bio was until after she was already her tech. She read it and was impressed even more than she had been. Yet Jemison was never "snooty." She'd greet McDougle—"Girl, how you doing?"—and then turn around to a fellow astronaut and be "super doctor scientist," using words McDougle had never heard before. Then Jemison would turn back and, without pause, continue her conversation with McDougle: "Girl, so what happened yesterday?"

Throughout the preparation time for the mission, Jemison would send little messages to her team to keep everyone in the loop about what was happening, which McDougle appreciated. She said Jemison never said thank you casually but always genuinely meant how important another team member had been to her success. She said Jemison kept what she called a "flight logbook." In it, she recorded the names of people key to the success of her mission. Nichelle Nichols was listed; Nikki Giovanni, a premier African American poet, was listed; and McDougle's name, too, was right there in Jemison's book.

McDougle has fond memories of Jemison's return to Earth. She was standing by, prepared to help in any way. She said most astronauts are not very strong stepping out of the orbiter because the return to Earth's gravity is hard on their bodies. They collapse into the techs' arms or need wheelchairs. But Jemison came walking toward McDougle "like she just came from the mall … That also shows you how strong she is."

McDougle also was the suit tech for Joan E. Higginbotham, the third African American woman in space. On "bring your child to work day," her kids practiced preparing Higginbotham. Again, the circles Jemison has spoken of looped—those children learned firsthand that they could be all they wanted to be.

"I just wanted it to be a good experience for her," McDougle told NASA of the final time she suited Jemison, right before the flight. It was crucial for Jemison, but it was special for McDougle, too, because, as she said, "I was excited about being a part of history."

The Leaders of Tomorrow

Jemison's Auburn University speech on "Daring Makes a Difference" had an immediate effect on at least two students present at the talk, as the school's newspaper, the *Plainsman*, reported. "She had to fight against so much. She was the front-runner for all of us," Crystal Downer, a student in osteopathic medicine, said.

Rakysia Rogers, a junior in political science, had been planning on going on to law school after finishing her undergraduate degree, but she welcomed Jemison's confirmation that everyone in the audience, including Rogers, could achieve what they wanted. "She was encouraging to me to not limit myself and to be confident even when society disagrees with me."

Ruthie Lyle-Cannon

At a presentation Jemison gave at Duke University in 2013, Ruthie Lyle-Cannon credited Jemison with inspiring her own career dreams. She earned her bachelor's degree in electrical engineering the year Jemison first went into space; Lyle-Cannon went on to become the first African American woman to earn a doctorate in electrical engineering from New York University, in 1998. She is considered a Master Inventor at IBM, one of the few women with that honor. As of 2012, she held 40 hardware and software patents, with another 150 pending approval,

Jemison at the 2017 Breakthrough Prize at NASA Ames Research Center.

which shows why she's considered such a high-level innovator.

Lyle-Cannon also benefited from special programs in high school and college. She was one of the first to be enrolled in an experimental program that offered high school students college-level engineering courses. Still, she didn't take any calculus and physics in high school. The Progress in Minority Engineering program in college helped Lyle-Cannon to fill in the gaps in her education.

Throughout her life, from when she read about Jemison as a teenager to when she caught the attention of IBM's vice president during a talk she gave to the National Action Council for Minorities in Engineering, Lyle-Cannon has known how beneficial good mentors and other support people can be. In turn, she now mentors and has brought up two female Master Inventors and participates in a week-long summer camp that brings middle school girls to IBM's North Carolina campus for experiential learning.

Those are examples of older students whose lives Jemison has affected, but through the many education-focused projects she's founded or supported, students of all ages have received her encouragement. The problem is bigger than poorly maintained school buildings, a lack of supplies, the eliminating of courses and programs, and overburdened teachers. The problem is also what society says by the allowing of those issues to persist: the message to students is that they and their education don't matter, don't deserve better, and have no future to prepare for. "Children live up or down to our expectations," Jemison said at Auburn University. "If we have a school that has no lab equipment, then those children never get the experience and will think we don't expect them to do well."

Analog Dreaming

Jemison is far from the only professional in the space industry who wants to see us push ourselves to travel farther into space. Her intense curiosity, technical knowledge, and leadership, even after she left NASA, in pushing experts to do more and in educating and encouraging the next generations all mean that she has contributed to the advancements her successors have made.

NASA's analog missions have been around since the Apollo era in order to test human responses to stresses similar to those in space. Analog missions occur on Earth in parts of the world based on physical similarities to the extreme environments of space. The missions have grown over the years, and now simulations push the boundaries that Jemison and many others have themselves nudged.

The thirteenth NASA Extreme Environment Mission Operations crew spent ten days underwater in 2007.

NASA's Desert Research and Technology Studies program happens in Arizona. This mission aims to test and improve equipment when used along rough terrain, in dust, and over periods of extreme temperature fluctuation.

The In-Situ Resource Utilization Demonstrations in Hawaii use local resources, like minerals, thermal gradients, and the unique blend of ice and sunlight, to complete exploration.

In the arctic desert of Canada, rocky, remote Haughton Crater is a great mimic of Mars. The Pavilion Lake Research Project, also in Canada, studies the fossilized freshwater microbialites found in Pavilion and Kelly Lakes. They were some of the earliest forms of life on Earth, and understanding them can help us understand life elsewhere.

Making Tents from Parachutes

Stephanie Wilson, the second African American woman in space, gave a TEDx talk in 2012 on astronaut training. Some people start training with military experience, but especially for those who come from the civilian world, this training offers a lot of new information and experiences.

Trainees learn land and water survival in case their shuttles crash down in unexpected places, including how to build tents from their parachutes, weave fishing nets from the parachute cords, and start a fire with nothing but flint. They have ejection seat training—without actually being ejected, Wilson was quick to clarify. Simulations are key for astronauts to learn what to do in situations so scary that NASA doesn't want to intentionally subject the astronauts to them. For example, in an unplanned water landing, astronauts must remember that their parachutes will drag them under the water. NASA trainers drag the astronauts behind a boat to simulate that situation, teaching them to detach their parachutes before the parachute drags them underwater. Some situations simply have to be simulated. For example, until astronauts are in space, they can't experience the feeling of space. But they can get a sense of weightlessness even while still on Earth. By walking through a very deep pool called the neutral buoyancy trainer, Jemison explained in an interview with Scholastic, they practice using their extravehicular activity suits, the big white spacewalking suits. They remain neutrally buoyant, neither floating nor sinking: "weightless." These suits also happen to weigh 250 pounds (113 kg). As Wilson said, aerospace work is "one of the only fields where you have to have help putting on your pants."

All astronauts, even those not from the military, fly T-38s and practice using the military-standard instruments and supplemental oxygen units because they sometimes fly to 45,000 feet (13,700 m). The KC-135 aircraft flies astronauts in a series of parabolic flight paths, at the tops of the loops releasing its passenger into twenty seconds of weightlessness within the plane. "It's like a big roller coaster," Jemison said. Or it's the Vomit Comet, as Wilson said the astronauts call the plane.

Though the astronauts train mostly at the Johnson Space Center in Houston, they do take field trips. They travel to the Midwest to conduct geological training, identifying and collecting rock and soil, practicing for when some of them will be assigned to take samples in space. And after two years on Earth, they travel to the International Space Station, 220 miles (354 km) above ground, for more training.

NEEMO, NASA's Extreme Environment Mission Operations, 62 feet (19 m) down in the Atlantic Ocean off of the Florida Keys, happens in Aquarius, sort of the deep-sea version of the International Space Station. "The stuff we are looking at in terms

Walking in water helps astronauts experience what it's like to walk in space.

of technique and modes of operating are things that they will look at years from now when we eventually make our way out to further destinations like Mars or [Mars's moon] Phobos or an asteroid," Serena Aunon, a NASA astronaut who was sent to Aquarius for two weeks in 2015, said. "When you look at the science we are trying to complete, there are not many places you can test it out. Under the sea is one of those missions."

The European Space Agency (ESA) has its own analog-type programs—for one, their space explorers live in uncharted cave systems for a week.

Space on Earth

It can be said that since Jemison participated in the space program, she has been part of its overall success, and that has led to improvements in life here on Earth.

As a result of work by NASA scientists, we have light-emitting diodes (LEDs) that can help human health. NASA uses LEDs as light for growing plants in space, and that technology has led to the LED unit WARP 10, which promotes muscle relaxation and increases local blood circulation, relieving muscle and joint pain. Space robots have become models for artificial limbs for humans.

NASA measures the temperature of stars and planets in a way that medical professionals have adapted to measure the temperature of particularly vulnerable patients, like newborns and those who are incapacitated.

Thanks to the NASA Langley Research Center's Safety Grooving research program, safety grooving, the grooves originally designed to reduce aircraft skidding on wet runways, is now also used on many of America's highways. The grooves

Stephanie Wilson

Stephanie Wilson was the second African American woman into space, fourteen years after Jemison's first flight. Born in Boston in 1966 and educated at Harvard and the University of Texas at Austin before joining NASA, Wilson was one of 43 astronauts selected out of 2,500 applicants to NASA's 1996 class. Though she got her start in the space program only four years after Jemison's pioneering flight, the bulk of Wilson's work happened in the twenty-first century. Her three space missions were in 2006, 2007, and 2010.

On her 2007 mission, Wilson was instrumental in organizing an unexpected spacewalk to repair and reattach a solar array. On her 2010 mission, she was one of four female astronauts—the first mission with that many women in space at once.

Wilson credits Williams College astronomy professor Jay Pasachoff with giving her the idea to become an astronaut. As a girl on a "learn about a career" school assignment, Wilson met Pasachoff, who talked not only about being an astronomer but about dovetailing that with engineering. His time and expertise meant so much to Wilson that she's invited him to all three of her shuttle launches.

Stephanie Wilson was the second African American woman in space.

cut into the roads improve traction and also help wake up dozing drivers.

Goodyear developed a material five times stronger than steel for NASA to use in safely landing the Viking missions on Mars; they adapted the material to improve car tires.

The aluminum composite material developed by NASA for use on rocket casings is now also used for firefighters' lightweight breathing systems.

Foam used in aircraft crashes now is used for pillows and mattresses—memory foam.

After Black and Decker made a portable, self-contained drill for the Apollo missions, the company then turned the computer program they'd developed for optimizing the drill to creating a cordless mini vacuum—the dustbuster.

NASA's engineers are turning perspiration and urine into drinking water; this will help astronauts be self-sustaining on the moon or farther away, and it will also help people right here on Earth who don't have access to plentiful uncontaminated water.

As much as Jemison doesn't like to focus on the resistance she's known over her life, because she doesn't see it as the key to advancement, she also doesn't focus on her position as a pioneer or role model. If anything comes directly from the cracks she's made in the glass ceiling, she hopes that it is acknowledgment of the efforts everyone makes and energy to not rest in a space of "good enough." We haven't done enough; there is more work to do.

"My being involved in the space program probably looks to some people as an affirmation that we're moving ahead as a society," Jemison said, "but we can't just stop with one person, and we can't stop with just the space program. We need to have all the people's skills and talents developed."

Glossary

aerobatics Acrobatics performed in the air.

aeronautics The science or practice of air travel.

aerospace Technology and industry of flight both within Earth's atmosphere and beyond it.

astronaut A person trained by a spaceflight agency or program to be part of a spacecraft crew; from the Greek for "space sailor."

aviation The operation of an aircraft.

aviator A pilot of an aircraft.

barnstorming Airplane pilots flying passengers on short sightseeing trips or, later, performing in stunt flying exhibitions, popular in the rural Midwest around the 1920s.

cosmonaut The Russian name for "astronaut."

disenfranchisement The denial of a privilege or legal right, especially the right to vote.

International Space Station Spacecraft that orbits the earth 220 miles (354 km) above the planet. It's both a science lab and a home for astronauts spending a long time in space. Many countries collaborated to build it, so now they all are allowed to use it.

mission A planned set of tasks with an end goal; a shuttle trip into space is a mission.

NACA The National Advisory Committee for Aeronautics was a US federal agency started in 1915 as an advisory committee to coordinate aeronautical research. The US agency was dissolved after the formation of NASA in 1958.

NASA The National Aeronautics and Space Administration was established by President Dwight D. Eisenhower in 1958. The organization focuses its work in aeronautics, human exploration of space, science of Earth and the universe, and space technology.

orbiter The part of a shuttle where astronauts live and work.

program (or project) Mercury, Gemini, and Apollo were NASA's first three projects, or programs, which included multiple missions to reach their big goals, such as establishing space flight and landing on the moon. Constellation was a program that was supposed to put humans back on the moon by 2020, but it was canceled.

shuttle A vehicle that launches into space.

SLS Space Launch System, a space shuttle-derived expendable launch vehicle being designed by NASA. The first flight is scheduled to occur September 30, 2018.

space race Twentieth-century competition for space exploration supremacy between the United States and the Soviet Union.

STS Space Transportation System, the official name for the manned US space shuttle program. There were 133 successful flights and 2 failures, starting with the first crewed flight, STS-1, on April 12, 1981, and ending with STS-135 on July 21, 2011.

trajectory The path of an object moving through space.

Chronology

1956 Mae C. Jemison is born in Decatur, Alabama.

1959 Jemison family moves to Chicago, Illinois.

1963 Valentina Tereshkova becomes first woman in space.

1973 Jemison graduates from Morgan Park High School in Chicago.

1977 Graduates with a BS in chemical engineering and a BA in African and Afro-American studies from Stanford University in California.

1980 Arnaldo Tamayo Méndez becomes first person of African descent to go into space.

1981 Graduates with a medical degree from Cornell University Medical School in New York.

1983 Joins the Peace Corps and serves for two years as a medical officer in Liberia and Sierra Leone. Sally Ride becomes the first American woman in space.

1985 Works as a physician in Los Angeles, California.

1987 Jemison is selected by NASA to join the astronaut corps.

1988 Essence Science and Technology Award winner.

1990 Gamma Sigma Woman of the Year.

1992 First African American woman in space. Receives the Ebony Black Achievement Award and the Johnson Publications Black Achievement Trailblazers Award. The Mae C. Jemison Science and Space Museum is named at Wilbur Wright Junior College in Chicago.

1993 Jemison resigns from NASA and founds the Jemison Group. She is inducted into the National Women's Hall of Fame and National Medical Association Hall of Fame. Becomes a professor of environmental studies at Dartmouth College. Appears in an episode of *Start Trek: The Next Generation.*

1994 Director, Jemison Institute for Advancing Technology in Developing Countries, Dartmouth.

1999 Founds the BioSentient Corp; is named Andrew D. White professor-at-large at Cornell University.

2004 Inducted in the International Space Hall of Fame.

2011 Appears in the TV film *No Gravity.*

2013 Retires from teaching full time.

2016 Cuts the ribbon on namesake high school in Huntsville, Alabama.

2017 LEGO announces Jemison will be featured as one of the figurines in its "Women of NASA" set.

Further Information

Books

Jemison, Mae. *Find Where the Wind Goes: Moments from My Life.* New York: Scholastic Press, 2001.

Paul, Richard, and Steven Moss. *We Could Not Fail: The First African Americans in the Space Program.* Austin: University of Texas Press, 2015.

Shetterly, Margot Lee. *Hidden Figures: The American Dream and the Untold Story of the Black Women Mathematicians Who Helped Win the Space Race.* New York: Harper Collins Publishing, 2016.

Websites

The Earth We Share (TEWS)

http://www.jemisonfoundation.org/international.htm

Mae Jemison's four-week international science camp is for middle school and high school students.

The Shuttle

https://www.nasa.gov/externalflash/the_shuttle/#fragment-1

Click through interactive guides to Space Transportation System missions and learn more about NASA shuttles.

Women@NASA

https://women.nasa.gov

Learn more about the women working throughout NASA over the years.

Films

Hidden Figures
http://www.imdb.com/title/tt4846340
Read about the the hit movie telling the story of three African American female computers at NASA, based on Margot Lee Shetterly's book.

Teach Arts and Sciences Together
http://www.ted.com/talks/mae_jemison_on_teaching_arts_and_sciences_together
View Mae Jemison's 2002 TED Talk.

Bibliography

"Astronaut Mae Jemison Launches Diversity Series with Message of Daring and Imagination." School of Engineering and Applied Science, University of Virginia. Accessed January 9, 2017. http://enews.seas.virginia.edu/astronaut-mae-jemison-launches-diversity-series-with-message-of-daring-and-imagination.

"Astronaut Requirements." NASA. Last updated December 17, 2015. https://www.nasa.gov/audience/forstudents/postsecondary/features/F_Astronaut_Requirements.html.

"College of Engineering Alumna Dr. Jan Davis on UAH, Space, and Tomorrow's Astronauts." The University of Alabama in Huntsville, November 14, 2013. http://www.uah.edu/news/people/college-of-engineering-alumna-dr-jan-davis-on-uah-space-and-tomorrow-s-astronauts.

"Dorothy Vaughan." The Human Computer Project. Accessed January 8, 2017. http://thehumancomputerproject.com/women/dorothy-vaughan.

"Dr. Mae Jemison Interview." Scholastic, March 15, 2001. http://teacher.scholastic.com/space/mae_jemison/interview.htm.

"Former Administrator Charlie Bolden." NASA Leadership, January 20, 2017. https://www.nasa.gov/about/highlights/bolden_bio.html.

Gubert, Betty Kaplan, Miriam Sawyer, and Caroline M. Fannin. *Distinguished African Americans in Aviation and Space Science.* Westport, CT: Oryx Press, 2002. https://books.google.com/books?id=LY9TAAAAMAAJ.

"History of Marches and Mass Actions." National Organization for Women. Accessed January 8, 2017. http://now.org/about/history/history-of-marches-and-mass-actions.

"How NASA's Space Race Helped to Integrate the South." *Morning Edition,* NPR, May 6, 2015. http://www.npr.org/2015/05/06/404626521/we-could-not-fail-the-first-african-americans-in-the-space-program.

Jackson, Camille. "The Legacy of Lt. Uhura: Astronaut Mae Jemison on Race in Space." *Duke Today,* October 28, 2013. https://today.duke.edu/2013/10/maejemison.

Jemison, Mae. "The Space Age, Race and a Quiet Revolution." *Huffington Post,* February 28, 2014. http://www.huffingtonpost.com/dr-mae-jemison/the-space-age-race-and-a-quiet-revolution_b_4875029.html?1393607865.

Kreider, Rose M., and Diana B. Elliott. "Historical Changes in Stay-at-Home Mothers: 1969 to 2009." Fertility and Family Statistics Branch, US Census Bureau. Presented at the American Sociological Association 2010 annual meetings, Atlanta, GA. https://www.census.gov/hhes/families/files/ASA2010_Kreider_Elliott.pdf.

"Mae Jemison." The Secret Life of Scientists, PBS. Accessed January 8, 2017. http://www.pbs.org/wgbh/nova/blogs/secretlife/space-science/mae-jemison.

Makers.com. Accessed January 9, 2017. http://www.makers.com.

"Meet a Super Scientists!" Scholastic, February 2001. http://teacher.scholastic.com/space/mae_jemison/index.htm.

Petrilla, Molly. "Meet the First Woman of Color to Go into Space." *Fortune.* Last updated September 14, 2015. http://fortune.com/2015/09/12/first-woman-of-color-in-space.

Rybarczyk, Tom. "Charlie Jemison, 78." *Chicago Tribune,* November 27, 2004. http://articles.chicagotribune.com/2004-11-27/news/0411270165_1_maintenance-engineer-roofer-morgan-park.

Sharon Caples McDougle, interviewed by Jennifer Ross-Nazzal. NASA Johnson Space Center Oral History Project, July 9, 2010. http://www.jsc.nasa.gov/history/oral_histories/McDougleSC/McDougleSC_7-9-10.htm.

"The Simple Truth About the Gender Pay Gap (Fall 2016)." AAUW. Accessed January 8, 2017. http://www.aauw.org/research/the-simple-truth-about-the-gender-pay-gap.

"Space Shuttle Overview: Endeavour." NASA. Accessed January 9, 2017. https://www.nasa.gov/centers/kennedy/shuttleoperations/orbiters/endeavour-info.html.

"Star Trek's Uhura Reflects on MLK Encounter." *Tell Me More*, January 17, 2011. http://www.npr.org/2011/01/17/132942461/Star-Treks-Uhura-Reflects-On-MLK-Encounter.

Stone, Tanya Lee. *Almost Astronauts: 13 Women Who Dared to Dream.* Somerville, MA: Candlewick Press, 2009. https://books.google.com/books/about/Almost_Astronauts.html?id=zLuPPEWq4GMC.

Index

About the Author

Kristin Thiel is a writer and editor. Her first book with Cavendish Square was on Dorothy Hodgkin, a Nobel Prize–winning chemist and pioneer in X-ray crystallography. She has worked on many of the books in the So, You Want to Be A ... series (Aladdin/ Beyond Words), which offers career guidance for kids. She was the lead writer on a report for her city about funding for high school dropout prevention. Thiel has judged YA book contests and helped start a Kids Voting USA affiliate. She has been a substitute teacher in grades K–12 and managed before-school and after-school literacy programs for AmeriCorps VISTA. Like thousands of other schoolchildren excited to see a teacher go into space, she watched the *Challenger* shuttle break apart on live television. But she agrees with Jemison that, overall, the adventure is worth any risk. She would not say no to a tall glass of Tang and a bowl of freeze-dried space ice cream.

$31.95

LONGWOOD PUBLIC LIBRARY
800 Middle Country Road
Middle Island, NY 11953
(631) 924-6400
longwoodlibrary.org

LIBRARY HOURS

Monday-Friday	9:30 a.m. - 9:00 p.m.
Saturday	9:30 a.m. - 5:00 p.m.
Sunday (Sept-June)	1:00 p.m. - 5:00 p.m.